To the Instructor

Thank you for your interest in the Townsend Press vocabulary series—the most widely-used vocabulary books on the college market today. Our goal in this series has been to produce nothing less than excellent books at nothing more than reasonable prices.

About the Book

Notice that the introduction to students (page 1) immediately makes clear to them just why vocabulary study is important. Students are motivated to learn by the four compelling kinds of evidence for word study. The back cover as well convinces students that "a solid vocabulary is a source of power."

You may want to look then at the preface, starting on page vii, which describes in detail the nine distinctive features of the book.

You'll see that a second color is used in the text to make the material as inviting as possible. You'll note, too, that while each chapter takes up only four pages, those pages contain a great deal of hands-on practice to help ensure that students master each word. And you'll find that the practice materials themselves are far more carefully done, and more appealing, than the run-of-the-mill items you typically find in a skills text. The quality and interest level of the content will help students truly learn the words, without either boring them or insulting their intelligence.

Supplements to the Book

Adding to the value of *Improving Vocabulary Skills, Short Version*, which has a net price of only $7.40, is the quality of the supplements:

• An *Instructor's Edition*, which you hold in your hand. The Instructor's Edition is identical to the student text except that it includes (in *italic type*) the answers to all of the practices and tests.

• A combined *Instructor's Manual and Test Bank*, free with adoptions of 20 or more copies. This booklet contains a general vocabulary placement test as well as a pretest and a posttest for the book and for each of the five units in the text. It also includes teaching guidelines, suggested syllabi, an answer key, and an additional mastery test for each chapter.

• A comprehensive series of IBM or Macintosh *computer disks*, which provide a general placement test and up to four additional tests for each vocabulary chapter in the book. Free with adoptions of 200 or more copies, the disks contain a number of user- and instructor-friendly features, including brief explanations of answers, a sound option, frequent mention of the user's first name, a running score at the bottom of the screen, and a record-keeping file.

Adopters of the book can obtain any of these supplements by calling our toll-free number, 1-800-772-6410, or by writing or faxing Townsend Press at the numbers shown on page iv.

(Continues on next page)

New Features of the Book

Among the changes in a book that has undergone significant revision are the following:

- Each chapter now begins with a multiple-choice format that gets students interacting immediately with each word.

- To provide more review and reinforcement, most of the words in each chapter are repeated in context in later chapters of the book. Repeated words are marked with a small circle (°) and appear in Sentence Check 2 and the Final Check.

- The print in the book has been enlarged, a pronunciation key now appears on the inside front cover, a crossword puzzle has been added as a unit review, and the introduction to the book has been expanded to include an explanation of the different types of context clues.

- Answer spaces can now be marked either with the word itself or with a number or letter—so that a Scantron machine or answer key can be used for easy grading.

A Comprehensive Vocabulary Program

There are seven books in the Townsend Press vocabulary series:

- *Groundwork for a Better Vocabulary, 2/e* (reading level 5–8)
- *Building Vocabulary Skills, 2/e* (reading level 7–9)
- *Improving Vocabulary Skills, 2/e* (reading level 9–11)
- *Advancing Vocabulary Skills, 2/e* (reading level 11–13)
- *Building Vocabulary Skills, Short Version, 2/e* (reading level 7–9)
- *Improving Vocabulary Skills, Short Version, 2/e* (reading level 9–11)
- *Advancing Vocabulary Skills, Short Version, 2/e* (reading level 11–13)

Note that the short versions of the three books are limited to 200 words, as opposed to the 260 words and 40 word parts in each of the long versions. For some students and classes, the short versions of the book will provide an easier, more manageable approach to vocabulary development.

IMPROVING VOCABULARY SKILLS

SHORT VERSION / Second Edition

SHERRIE L. NIST
UNIVERSITY OF GEORGIA

CAROLE MOHR

TOWNSEND PRESS   Marlton, NJ 08053

Books in the Townsend Press Vocabulary Series:

GROUNDWORK FOR A BETTER VOCABULARY, 2/e
BUILDING VOCABULARY SKILLS, 2/e
IMPROVING VOCABULARY SKILLS, 2/e
ADVANCING VOCABULARY SKILLS, 2/e
BUILDING VOCABULARY SKILLS, SHORT VERSION, 2/e
IMPROVING VOCABULARY SKILLS, SHORT VERSION, 2/e
ADVANCING VOCABULARY SKILLS, SHORT VERSION, 2/e

Books in the Townsend Press Reading Series:

GROUNDWORK FOR COLLEGE READING, 2/e
KEYS TO BETTER COLLEGE READING
TEN STEPS TO BUILDING COLLEGE READING SKILLS, FORM A, 2/e
TEN STEPS TO BUILDING COLLEGE READING SKILLS, FORM B, 2/e
TEN STEPS TO IMPROVING COLLEGE READING SKILLS, 2/e
IMPROVING READING COMPREHENSION SKILLS
TEN STEPS TO ADVANCING COLLEGE READING SKILLS, 2/e

Supplements Available for Most Books:

Instructor's Edition
Instructor's Manual, Test Bank, and Computer Guide
Set of Computer Disks (IBM or Macintosh)

Copyright © 1997 by Townsend Press, Inc.
Printed in the United States of America
ISBN 0-944210-34-1
9 8 7 6 5 4 3 2 1

Send book orders to:
Townsend Press
1038 Industrial Drive
West Berlin, New Jersey 08091

For even faster service, call us at our toll-free number:
1-800-772-6410

Or FAX your request to:
1-609-753-0649

ISBN 0-944210-34-1

Contents

Note: For ease of reference, the title of the selection that closes each chapter is included.

UNIT FOUR

APPENDIXES

Preface

The problem is all too familiar: *students just don't know enough words*. Reading, writing, and content teachers agree that many students' vocabularies are inadequate for the demands of courses. Weak vocabularies limit students' understanding of what they read and the clarity and depth of what they write.

The purpose of the Townsend Press vocabulary series is to provide a solid, workable answer to the vocabulary problem. The short version of the series consists of three books, each of which *teaches* 200 important words. Within each book are twenty chapters, with ten words in each chapter. Here are the distinctive features of *Improving Vocabulary Skills, Short Version, Second Edition*:

1 **An intensive words-in-context approach.** Studies show that students learn words best by reading them repeatedly in different contexts, not through rote memorization. The book gives students an intensive in-context experience by presenting each word in six different contexts. Each chapter takes students through a productive sequence of steps:

- Students infer the meaning of each word by considering two sentences in which it appears and then choosing from multiple-choice options.
- On the basis of their inferences, students identify each word's meaning in a matching test. They are then in a solid position to deepen their knowledge of a word.
- Finally, they strengthen their understanding of a word by applying it three times: in two sentence practices and in a selection practice.

Each encounter with a word brings it closer to becoming part of the student's permanent word bank.

2 **Abundant practice.** Along with extensive practice in each chapter, there are a crossword puzzle and a set of unit tests at the end of every five-chapter unit. The puzzle and tests reinforce students' knowledge of the words in each chapter. In addition, most chapters reuse several words from earlier chapters (such repeated words are marked with small circles), allowing for more reinforcement. Last, there are supplementary tests in the *Test Bank* and the computer disks that accompany the book. All this practice means that students learn in the surest possible way: by working closely and repeatedly with each word.

3 **Controlled feedback.** The opening activity in each chapter gives students three multiple-choice options to help them decide on the meaning of a given word. The multiple-choice options also help students to complete the matching test that is the second activity of each chapter. A limited answer key at the back of the book then provides answers for the third activity in the chapter. All these features enable students to take an active role in their own learning.

4 Focus on essential words. A good deal of time and research went into selecting the 200 words featured in the book. Word frequency lists were consulted, along with lists in a wide range of vocabulary books. In addition, the authors and editors each prepared their own lists. A computer was used to help in the consolidation of the many word lists. A long process of group discussion then led to final decisions about the words that would be most helpful for students on a basic reading level.

5 Appealing content. Dull practice materials work against learning. On the other hand, meaningful, lively, and at times even funny sentences and selections can spark students' attention and thus enhance their grasp of the material. For this reason, a great deal of effort was put into creating sentences and selections with both widespread appeal and solid context support. We have tried throughout to make the practice materials truly enjoyable for teachers and students alike. Look, for example, at the selection on page 19 that closes the third chapter of this book.

6 Clear format. The book has been designed so that its very format contributes to the learning process. Each chapter consists of two two-page spreads. In the first two-page spread (the first such spread is on pages 8–9), students can easily refer to all ten words in context while working on the matching test, which provides a clear meaning for each word. In the second two-page spread, students can refer to a box that shows all ten words while they work through the fill-in activities on these pages.

7 Supplementary materials.

a A convenient *Instructor's Edition* is available at no charge to instructors using the book. It is identical to the student book except that it contains answers to all of the activities and tests.

b A combined *Instructor's Manual and Test Bank* is also offered at no charge to instructors who have adopted the book. This booklet contains a general vocabulary placement test as well as a pretest and a posttest for the book and for each of the four units in the text. It also includes teaching guidelines, suggested syllabi, an answer key, and an additional mastery test for each chapter.

c A *comprehensive series of computer disks* also accompanies the book. Free to adopters of 200 or more copies, these disks provide up to four tests for each vocabulary chapter in the book. The disks include a number of user- and instructor-friendly features: brief explanations of answers, a sound option, frequent mention of the user's first name, a running score at the bottom of the screen, a record-keeping file, and (in the case of the Macintosh disks) actual pronunciation of each word.

  Probably in no other area of reading instruction is the computer more useful than in reinforcing vocabulary. This vocabulary program takes full advantage of the computer's unique capabilities and motivational appeal. Here's how the program works:

- Students are tested on the ten words in a chapter, with each word in a sentence context different from any in the book itself.

- After students answer each question, they receive immediate feedback: The computer tells if a student is right or wrong and why, frequently using the student's first name and providing a running score.

- When the test is over, the computer supplies a test score and—this especially is what is unique about this program—a chance to retest on the specific words the student got wrong. For example, if a student misses four items on a test, the retest provides four different sentences that test just those four words. Students then receive a score for this special retest. What is so valuable about this, of course, is that the computer gives students added practice in the words they most need to review.

- In addition, the computer offers a second, more challenging test in which students must identify the meanings of the chapter words without benefit of context. This test is a final check that students have really learned the words. And, again, there is the option of a retest, tailor-made to recheck only those words missed on the first definition test.

By the end of this program, students' knowledge of each word in the chapter will have been carefully reinforced. And this reinforcement will be the more effective for having occurred in an electronic medium that especially engages today's students.

To obtain a copy of any of the above materials, instructors may write to the Reading Editor, Townsend Press, Pavilions at Greentree—408, Marlton, NJ 08053. Alternatively, instructors may call our toll-free number: 1-800-772-6410.

8 Realistic pricing. As with the first edition, the goal has been to offer the highest possible quality at the best possible price. While *Improving Vocabulary Skills* is comprehensive enough to serve as a primary text, its modest price also makes it an inexpensive supplement.

9 One in a sequence of books. The most basic book in the Townsend Press vocabulary series is *Groundwork for a Better Vocabulary*. It is followed by the three main books in the series: *Building Vocabulary Skills* (also a basic text), *Improving Vocabulary Skills* (an intermediate text), and *Advancing Vocabulary Skills* (a more advanced text). There are also short versions of these three books, including this book, *Improving Vocabulary Skills, Short Version, Second Edition*. Suggested grade levels for the books are included in the *Instructor's Manual*. Together, the books can help create a vocabulary foundation that will make any student a better reader, writer, and thinker.

NOTES ON THE SECOND EDITION

A number of changes have been made to the book.

- Instead of an opening preview, each chapter now begins with a new format that uses a multiple-choice question to get students interacting immediately with each word. Teachers' and students' responses to this change have been extremely favorable.

- For ease of grading, including the use of Scantron machines, answer spaces can now be marked either with the letter or number of the word or with the word itself.

- The print in the book has been enlarged, a pronunciation key now appears on the inside front cover, a crossword puzzle has been added as a unit review, and the introduction to the book has been expanded. In addition, hundreds of changes have been made throughout the book to make each practice item work as clearly and effectively as possible.

- Thanks to feedback from reviewers and users, many of the words in each chapter are now repeated in context in later chapters (and marked with small circles). Such repetition provides students with even more review and reinforcement.

ACKNOWLEDGMENTS

We are grateful for the enthusiastic comments provided by users of the Townsend Press vocabulary books over the life of the first edition. Particular thanks go to the following reviewers for their many helpful suggestions: Barbara Brennan Culhane, Nassau Community College; Carol Dietrick, Miami-Dade Community College; Larry Falxa, Ventura College; Jacquelin Hanselman, Hillsborough Community College; Shiela P. Kerr, Florida Community College at Jacksonville; John M. Kopec, Boston University; Belinda E. Smith, Wake Technical Community College; Daniel Snook, Montcalm Community College; and William Walcott, Montgomery College. We appreciate as well the editing work of Eliza Comodromos and the design, editing, and proofreading skills of the multi-talented Janet M. Goldstein. Finally, we dedicate this book to the memory of our computer programmer, Terry Hutchison.

Sherrie L. Nist   *Carole Mohr*

Introduction

WHY VOCABULARY DEVELOPMENT COUNTS

You have probably often heard it said, "Building vocabulary is important." Maybe you've politely nodded in agreement and then forgotten the matter. But it would be fair for you to ask, "*Why* is vocabulary development important? Provide some evidence." Here are four compelling kinds of evidence.

1 Common sense tells you what many research studies have shown as well: vocabulary is a basic part of reading comprehension. Simply put, if you don't know enough words, you are going to have trouble understanding what you read. An occasional word may not stop you, but if there are too many words you don't know, comprehension will suffer. The content of textbooks is often challenge enough; you don't want to work as well on understanding the words that express that content.

2 Vocabulary is a major part of almost every standardized test, including reading achievement tests, college entrance exams, and armed forces and vocational placement tests. Test developers know that vocabulary is a key measure of both one's learning and one's ability to learn. It is for this reason that they include a separate vocabulary section as well as a reading comprehension section. The more words you know, then, the better you are likely to do on such important tests.

3 Studies have indicated that students with strong vocabularies are more successful in school. And one widely known study found that a good vocabulary, more than any other factor, was common to people enjoying successful careers in life. Words are in fact the tools not just of better reading, but of better writing, speaking, listening, and thinking as well. The more words you have at your command, the more effective your communication can be, and the more influence you can have on the people around you.

4 In today's world, a good vocabulary counts more than ever. Far fewer people work on farms or in factories. Far more are in jobs that provide services or process information. More than ever, words are the tools of our trade: words we use in reading, writing, listening, and speaking. Furthermore, experts say that workers of tomorrow will be called on to change jobs and learn new skills at an ever-increasing pace. The keys to survival and success will be the abilities to communicate skillfully and learn quickly. A solid vocabulary is essential for both of these skills.

Clearly, the evidence is overwhelming that building vocabulary is crucial. The question then becomes, "What is the best way of going about it?"

WORDS IN CONTEXT: THE KEY TO VOCABULARY DEVELOPMENT

Memorizing lists of words is a traditional method of vocabulary development. However, a person is likely to forget such memorized lists quickly. Studies show that to master a word, you must see and use it in various contexts. By working actively and repeatedly with a word, you greatly increase the chance of really learning it.

The following activity will make clear how this book is organized and how it uses a words-in-context approach. Answer the questions or fill in the missing words in the spaces provided.

Inside Front Cover and Contents

Turn to the inside front cover.

- The inside front cover provides a ____*pronunciation guide*____ that will help you pronounce all the vocabulary words in the book.

Now turn to the table of contents on pages v-vi.

- How many chapters are in the book? ___*20*___

- Three short sections follow the last chapter. The first of these sections provides a limited answer key, the second gives helpful information on using _____*the dictionary*_____, and the third is an index of the 200 words in the book.

Vocabulary Chapters

Turn to Chapter 1 on pages 8–11. This chapter, like all the others, consists of five parts:

- The *first part* of the chapter, on pages 8–9, is titled _____*Ten Words in Context*_____.

    The left-hand column lists the ten words. Under each **boldfaced** word is its ____*pronunciation*____ (in parentheses). For example, the pronunciation of *absolve* is _____*ăb-zŏlv′*_____. For a guide to pronunciation, see the inside front cover as well as "Dictionary Use" on page 129.

    Below the pronunciation guide for each word is its part of speech. The part of speech shown for *absolve* is ____*verb*____. The vocabulary words in this book are mostly nouns, adjectives, and verbs. **Nouns** are words used to name something—a person, place, thing, or idea. Familiar nouns include *boyfriend, city, hat,* and *truth*. **Adjectives** are words that describe nouns, as in the following word pairs: *former* boyfriend, *large* city, *red* hat, *whole* truth. All of the **verbs** in this book express an action of some sort. They tell what someone or something is doing. Common verbs include *sing, separate, support,* and *imagine*.

    To the right of each word are two sentences that will help you understand its meaning. In each sentence, the **context**—the words surrounding the boldfaced word—provides clues you can use to figure out the definition. There are four common types of context clues—examples, synonyms, antonyms, and the general sense of the sentence. Each is briefly described below.

    1 Examples

      A sentence may include examples that reveal what an unfamiliar word means. For instance, take a look at the following sentence from Chapter 1 for the word *eccentric*:

        Bruce is quite **eccentric**. For example, he lives in a circular house and rides to work on a motorcycle, in a three-piece suit.

      The sentences provide two examples of what makes Bruce eccentric. The first is that he lives in a circular house. The second is that he rides to work on a motorcycle while wearing a three-piece suit. What do these two examples have in common? The answer to that question will tell you what *eccentric* means. Look at the answer choices below, and in the answer space provided, write the letter of the one you feel is correct.

___ *Eccentric* means   a. ordinary.   b. odd.   c. careful.

Both of the examples given in the sentences about Bruce tell us that he is unusual, or odd. So if you wrote *b*, you chose the correct answer.

2 Synonyms

Synonyms are words that mean the same or almost the same as another word. For example, the words *joyful, happy*, and *delighted* are synonyms—they all mean about the same thing. Synonyms serve as context clues by providing the meaning of an unknown word that is nearby. The sentence below from Chapter 1 provides a synonym clue for *amiable*.

At first, our history teacher doesn't seem very friendly, but once you get to know her, she shows her **amiable** side.

Instead of using *amiable* twice, the author used a synonym in the first part of the sentence. Find that synonym, and then choose the letter of the correct answer from the choices below.

___ *Amiable* means   a. intelligent.   b. uncaring.   c. good-natured.

The author uses two words to discuss one of the history teacher's qualities: *friendly* and *amiable*. This tells us that *amiable* must be another way of saying *friendly*. (The author could have written "she shows her *friendly* side.") Since *friendly* can also mean *good-natured*, the correct answer is *c*.

3 Antonyms

Antonyms are words with opposite meanings. For example, *help* and *harm* are antonyms, as are *work* and *rest*. Antonyms serve as context clues by providing the opposite meaning of an unknown word. For instance, the sentence below from Chapter 1 provides an antonym clue for the word *antagonist*.

In the ring, the two boxers were **antagonists**, but in their private lives they were good friends.

The author is contrasting the boxers' two different relationships, so we can assume that *antagonists* and *good friends* have opposite, or contrasting, meanings. Using that contrast as a clue, write the letter of the answer that you think best defines *antagonist*.

___ *Antagonist* means   a. a supporter.   b. an enemy.   c. an example.

The correct answer is *b*. Because *antagonist* is the opposite of *friend*, it must mean "enemy."

4 General Sense of the Sentence

Even when there is no example, synonym, or antonym clue in a sentence, you can still deduce the meaning of an unfamiliar word. For example, look at the sentence from Chapter 1 for the word *malign*.

That vicious Hollywood reporter often **maligns** movie stars, forever damaging their public images.

After studying the context carefully, you should be able to figure out what the reporter does to movie stars. That will be the meaning of *malign*. Write the letter of your choice.

___ *Malign* means   a. to praise.   b. to recognize.   c. to speak ill of.

Since the sentence calls the reporter "vicious" and says she damages public images, it is logical to conclude that she says negative things about movie stars. Thus answer *c* is correct.

By looking closely at the pair of sentences provided for each word, as well as the answer choices, you should be able to decide on the meaning of a word. As you figure out each meaning, you are working actively with the word. You are creating the groundwork you need to understand and to remember the word. *Getting involved with the word and developing a feel for it, based upon its use in context, is the key to word mastery.*

It is with good reason, then, that the directions at the top of page 8 tell you to use the context to figure out each word's _____*meaning*_____. Doing so deepens your sense of the word and prepares you for the next activity.

- The *second part* of the chapter, on page 9, is titled _____*Matching Words with Definitions*_____.

According to research, it is not enough to see a word in context. At a certain point, it is helpful as well to see the meaning of a word. The matching test provides that meaning, but it also makes you look for and think about that meaning. In other words, it continues the active learning that is your surest route to learning and remembering a word.

Note the caution that follows the test. Do not proceed any further until you are sure that you know the correct meaning of each word as used in context.

Keep in mind that a word may have more than one meaning. In fact, some words have quite a few meanings. (If you doubt it, try looking up in a dictionary, for example, the word *make* or *draw*.) In this book, you will focus on one common meaning for each vocabulary word. However, many of the words have additional meanings. For example, in Chapter 9, you will learn that *devastate* means "to upset deeply," as in the sentence "The parents were devastated when they learned that their son had been arrested." If you then look up *devastate* in the dictionary, you will discover that it has another meaning—"to destroy," as in "The hurricane devastated much of Florida." After you learn one common meaning of a word, you will find yourself gradually learning its other meanings in the course of your school and personal reading.

- The *third part* of the chapter, on page 10, is titled _____*Sentence Check 1*_____.

Here are ten sentences that give you an opportunity to apply your understanding of the ten words. After inserting the words, check your answers in the limited key at the back of the book. Be sure to use the answer key as a learning tool only. Doing so will help you to master the words and to prepare for the last two activities and the unit tests, for which answers are not provided.

- The *fourth and fifth parts* of the chapter, on pages 10–11, are titled _____*Sentence Check 2*_____ and _____*Final Check*_____.

Each practice tests you on all ten words, giving you two more chances to deepen your mastery. In the fifth part, you have the context of an entire passage in which you can practice applying the words.

At the bottom of the last page of this chapter is a box where you can enter your score for the final two checks. These scores should also be entered into the vocabulary performance chart located on the inside back page of the book. To get your score, take 10% off for each item wrong. For example, 0 wrong = 100%, 1 wrong = 90%, 2 wrong = 80%, 3 wrong = 70%, 4 wrong = 60%, and so on.

You now know, in a nutshell, how to proceed with the words in each chapter. Make sure that you do each page very carefully. *Remember that as you work through the activities, you are learning the words.*

How many times in all will you use each word? If you look, you'll see that each chapter gives you the opportunity to work with each word six times. Each "impression" adds to the likelihood that the word will become part of your active vocabulary. You will have further opportunities to use the word in the crossword puzzle and unit tests that end each unit and on the computer disks that are available with the book.

In addition, many of the words are repeated in context in later chapters of the book. Such repeated words are marked with small circles. For example, which words from Chapter 1 are repeated in the Final Check on page 15 of Chapter 2?

_____*antagonist*_____   _____*amoral*_____

A FINAL THOUGHT

The facts are in. A strong vocabulary is a source of power. Words can make you a better reader, writer, speaker, thinker, and learner. They can dramatically increase your chances of success in school and in your job.

But words will not come automatically. They must be learned in a program of regular study. If you commit yourself to learning words, and you work actively and honestly with the chapters in this book, you will not only enrich your vocabulary—you will enrich your life as well.

Unit One

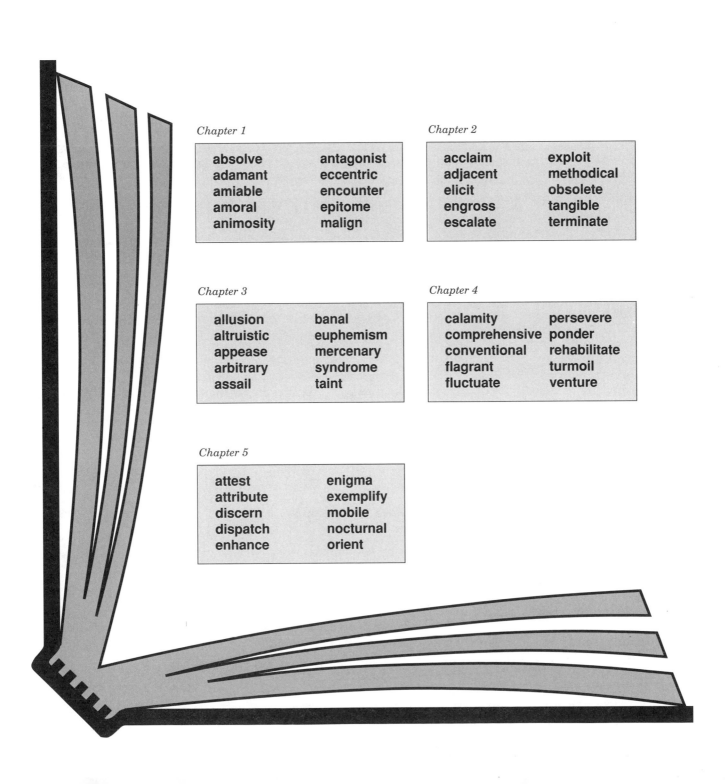

Chapter 1

absolve	antagonist
adamant	eccentric
amiable	encounter
amoral	epitome
animosity	malign

Chapter 2

acclaim	exploit
adjacent	methodical
elicit	obsolete
engross	tangible
escalate	terminate

Chapter 3

allusion	banal
altruistic	euphemism
appease	mercenary
arbitrary	syndrome
assail	taint

Chapter 4

calamity	persevere
comprehensive	ponder
conventional	rehabilitate
flagrant	turmoil
fluctuate	venture

Chapter 5

attest	enigma
attribute	exemplify
discern	mobile
dispatch	nocturnal
enhance	orient

CHAPTER
1

absolve	antagonist
adamant	eccentric
amiable	encounter
amoral	epitome
animosity	malign

Ten Words in Context

In the space provided, write the letter of the meaning closest to that of each **boldfaced** word. Use the context of the sentences to help you figure out each word's meaning.

1 **absolve**
(ăb-zŏlv′)
-verb

- Having insufficient evidence of his guilt, the jury had to **absolve** Mr. Melman of the murder.
- Accused of taking bribes, the mayor said, "In the end, I'll clear my name and be **absolved** of any wrongdoing."

_b_ _Absolve_ means   a. to accuse.   b. to clear of guilt.   c. to inform.

2 **adamant**
(ăd′ə-mənt)
-adjective

- Ron is **adamant** about not changing plans. He insists we still camp out even though the weather report now says it will be cold and rainy.
- **Adamant** in his support of gun control, Senator Keen won't give in to pressure from powerful opponents.

_a_ _Adamant_ means   a. firm.   b. uncertain.   c. flexible.

3 **amiable**
(ā′mē-ə-bəl)
-adjective

- My **amiable** dog greets both strangers and old friends with a happy yip and energetic tail-wagging.
- At first, our history teacher doesn't seem very friendly, but once you get to know her, she shows her **amiable** side.

_c_ _Amiable_ means   a. intelligent.   b. uncaring.   c. good-natured.

4 **amoral**
(ā-mŏr′əl)
-adjective

- Jerry is almost totally **amoral**. He cares only about making money and having fun and couldn't care less about right or wrong.
- A former president of Uganda, Idi Amin, was truly **amoral**. He jailed, tortured, and killed innocent opponents without the slightest feeling of guilt.

_c_ _Amoral_ means   a. cowardly.   b. lazy.   c. lacking ethical principles.

5 **animosity**
(ăn′ə-mŏs′ə-tē)
-noun

- I was shocked when Sandy said she hated Lionel. I'd never realized she felt such **animosity** toward him.
- Ill will between the two families goes back so many generations that nobody remembers what originally caused the **animosity**.

_a_ _Animosity_ means   a. strong dislike.   b. admiration.   c. great fear.

6 **antagonist**
(ăn-tăg′ə-nĭst)
-noun

- At the divorce hearing, the husband and wife were such bitter **antagonists** that it was hard to believe they had once loved each other.
- In the ring, the two boxers were **antagonists**, but in their private lives they were good friends.

_b_ _Antagonist_ means   a. a supporter.   b. an enemy.   c. an example.

8

7 **eccentric**
(ĭk-sĕn′trĭk)
-adjective

- Bruce is quite **eccentric**. For example, he lives in a circular house and rides to work on a motorcycle, in a three-piece suit.
- Florence Nightingale, the famous nursing reformer, had the **eccentric** habit of carrying a pet owl around in one of her pockets.

_b_ *Eccentric* means   a. ordinary.   b. odd.   c. careful.

8 **encounter**
(ĕn-koun′tər)
-verb

- I was surprised to **encounter** Matt in a supermarket in Los Angeles, since I thought he still lived in Chicago.
- I dislike returning to my small hometown, where I am likely to **encounter** people who knew me as a troubled kid.

_b_ *Encounter* means   a. to think of.   b. to forget.   c. to meet.

9 **epitome**
(ĭ-pĭt′ə-mē)
-noun

- To many, the **epitome** of cuteness is a furry, round-eyed puppy.
- The great ballplayer and civil rights leader Jackie Robinson was the **epitome** of both physical and moral strength.

_a_ *Epitome* means   a. a perfect model.   b. an opposite.   c. a main cause.

10 **malign**
(mə′līn)
-verb

- Stacy continually **maligns** her ex-husband. The way she describes him, you'd think he was a cross between a blockhead and a mass murderer.
- That vicious Hollywood reporter often **maligns** movie stars, forever damaging their public images.

_c_ *Malign* means   a. to praise.   b. to recognize.   c. to speak ill of.

Matching Words with Definitions

Following are definitions of the ten words. Clearly write or print each word next to its definition. The sentences above and on the previous page will help you decide on the meaning of each word.

1. _adamant_   Not giving in; stubborn
2. _amoral_   Lacking a moral sense; without principles
3. _eccentric_   Differing from what is customary; odd
4. _absolve_   To find innocent or blameless
5. _encounter_   To meet unexpectedly; come upon
6. _epitome_   A perfect or typical example of a general quality or type
7. _antagonist_   An opponent; one who opposes or competes
8. _animosity_   Bitter hostility
9. _malign_   To make evil and often untrue statements about; speak evil of
10. _amiable_   Good-natured; friendly and pleasant

CAUTION: Do not go any further until you are sure the above answers are correct. Then you can use the definitions to help you in the following practices. Your goal is eventually to know the words well enough so that you don't need to check the definitions at all.

➤ *Sentence Check 1*

Using the answer line provided, complete each item below with the correct word from the box. Use each word once.

| a. **absolve** | b. **adamant** | c. **amiable** | d. **amoral** | e. **animosity** |
| f. **antagonist** | g. **eccentric** | h. **encounter** | i. **epitome** | j. **malign** |

_____adamant_____ 1. Lilly was ___ in her belief that Sam was faithful. Even lipstick on his cheek didn't weaken her trust in him.

_____encounter_____ 2. My brothers had planned to meet in the restaurant, but they ___(e)d each other in the parking lot.

_____malign_____ 3. I'm tired of hearing the two candidates for governor ___ each other with stupid insults.

_____amiable_____ 4. Because he doesn't want to lose a sale, Mac remains polite and ___ even when he's annoyed with a customer.

_____amoral_____ 5. Some criminals are truly ___—they don't see that some actions are right and that others are wrong.

_____epitome_____ 6. The ___ of refreshment is drinking an ice-cold lemonade on a sizzling hot day.

_____absolve_____ 7. Jed was ___(e)d of stealing money from the company, but the damage the accusation did to his reputation remained.

_____antagonist_____ 8. The owners of the department store were always competing with each other. They acted more like ___s than partners.

_____animosity_____ 9. I avoid serious discussions with my sister because she shows great ___ toward me if I don't share her opinion.

_____eccentric_____ 10. Today it's not odd for females to learn carpentry, but when my mother went to high school, girls who took wood shop were considered ___.

NOTE: Now check your answers to these questions by turning to page 127. Going over the answers carefully will help you prepare for the next two practices, for which answers are not given.

➤ *Sentence Check 2*

Using the answer lines provided, complete each item below with **two** words from the box. Use each word once.

_____eccentric_____
_____encounter_____ 1–2. The ___ millionaire dressed so shabbily that anyone who ___(e)d him thought he was poor.

_____animosity_____
_____malign_____ 3–4. Hector feels such ___ toward his sister that he never says a single kind thing about her; he only ___s her.

_____ *adamant* _____   5–6. Since the congresswoman was ___ in opposing the nuclear power
_____ *antagonist* _____   plant, the plant's owners regarded her as their toughest ___.

_____ *amoral* _____   7–8. Wayne is so ___ that he doesn't even have the desire to be ___(e)d of
_____ *absolve* _____   guilt for all the times he has lied, cheated, and stolen.

_____ *epitome* _____   9–10. With his friendly air, good-natured laugh and generosity, Santa Claus is
_____ *amiable* _____   the ___ of the ___ grandfather.

➤*Final Check:* Joseph Palmer

Here is a final opportunity for you to strengthen your knowledge of the ten words. First read the following selection carefully. Then fill in each blank with a word from the box at the top of the previous page. (Context clues will help you figure out which word goes in which blank.) Use each word once.

In 1830, a Massachusetts farmer named Joseph Palmer moved to the city, only to find that people continually reacted to him with anger and hatred. Why? Palmer certainly wasn't a(n) (1)_____ *amoral* _____ man—no, he had a strong sense of right and wrong. He was a friendly and (2)_____ *amiable* _____ person as well. And on the whole, Palmer was the (3)_____ *epitome* _____ of a normal citizen, living a typical life with his family. Yet his neighbors crossed to the other side of the street when they (4)_____ *encounter* _____(e)d him. Children insulted Palmer and sometimes threw stones at him. Grown men hurled rocks through the windows of his house. Even the local minister (5)_____ *malign* _____(e)d Palmer, telling the congregation that Palmer admired only himself.

One day, four men carrying scissors and a razor attacked Palmer and threw him to the ground. Pulling out a pocketknife, Palmer fought back, slashing at their legs. His (6)_____ *antagonist* _____s fled. Afterward, Palmer was the one arrested and jailed. While in jail he was attacked two more times. Both times, he fought his way free. After a year—although his accusers still wouldn't (7)_____ *absolve* _____ him of guilt—he was released.

Palmer had won. The cause of all the (8)_____ *animosity* _____ and abuse had been his long, flowing beard. Palmer, (9)_____ *adamant* _____ to the end, had refused to shave.

Thirty years after Palmer's difficulties, it was no longer (10)_____ *eccentric* _____ to wear whiskers. Among the many who wore beards then was the President of the United States, Abraham Lincoln.

Scores	Sentence Check 2 ___%	Final Check ___%

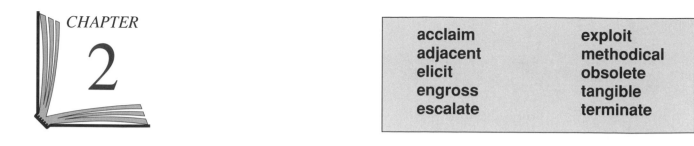

CHAPTER 2

acclaim	exploit
adjacent	methodical
elicit	obsolete
engross	tangible
escalate	terminate

Ten Words in Context

In the space provided, write the letter of the meaning closest to that of each **boldfaced** word. Use the context of the sentences to help you figure out each word's meaning.

1 acclaim
(ə-klām')
-noun

- Any subway system that is clean, quiet, and safe deserves **acclaim**.
- Although Vincent Van Gogh is now considered a genius, the artist received little **acclaim** in his lifetime.

_b_ *Acclaim* means   a. criticism.   b. praise.   c. change.

2 adjacent
(ə-jā'sənt)
-adjective

- Because their desks are **adjacent**, Jeff and Kellie often exchange looks and comments.
- If you keep your dishes in a cupboard that's **adjacent** to the dishwasher, you won't have to walk when putting away the clean dishes.

_a_ *Adjacent* means   a. close.   b. similar.   c. separated.

3 elicit
(ĭ-lĭs'ĭt)
-verb

- Elizabeth Taylor's violet eyes always **elicit** admiration and wonder.
- Wes is such a troublemaker in Mrs. Turner's class that his late arrival one day **elicited** this sharp comment from her: "In your case, Wes, never is better than late."

_c_ *Elicit* means   a. to stop.   b. to follow.   c. to bring out.

4 engross
(ĕn'grōs')
-verb

- The suspenseful TV movie so **engrossed** Bryan that he didn't even budge when he was called to dinner.
- The fascinating single-file march of black ants along the sidewalk **engrossed** me for several minutes.

_a_ *Engross* means   a. to hold the interest of.   b. to disgust.   c. to bore.

5 escalate
(ĕs'kə-lāt')
-verb

- The fight between the two hockey players **escalated** into an all-out battle among members of both teams.
- "We need to **escalate** our fund-raising efforts," the theater manager said. "Otherwise, the company won't survive."

_a_ *Escalate* means   a. to expand.   b. to delay.   c. to weaken.

6 exploit
(ĕks-ploit')
-verb

- At the turn of the century, factory owners **exploited** children by making them work in terrible conditions for as many as eighteen hours a day.
- Ricky **exploited** his parents' absence by having a wild party at their home.

_b_ *Exploit* means   a. to forget.   b. to take advantage of.   c. to be sad about.

7 **methodical**
(mə-thŏd′ĭ-kəl)
-adjective
- A **methodical** way to store spices is to shelve them in alphabetical order.
- Joan is so **methodical** about her diet that she classifies the foods in each meal into different nutritional categories.

_c_ *Methodical* means   a. accidental.   b. out-of-date.   c. orderly.

8 **obsolete**
(ŏb′sə lēt′)
-adjective
- Word processors are so common now that they have made typewriters almost **obsolete**.
- In the United States, the automobile quickly made travel by horse and carriage **obsolete**.

_c_ *Obsolete* means   a. popular.   b. useful.   c. extinct.

9 **tangible**
(tăn′jə-bəl)
-adjective
- The sculptor loved making her ideas **tangible** by giving them form in metal and stone.
- Corn-chip crumbs, empty soda bottles, and dirty napkins were **tangible** evidence that a party had taken place the night before.

_b_ *Tangible* means   a. clever.   b. solid.   c. hidden.

10 **terminate**
(tûr′mə-nāt)
-verb
- The students waited impatiently for the bell to **terminate** Mr. Leeman's boring lecture.
- The referee should have **terminated** the boxing match when he first saw the weaker fighter losing the ability to defend himself.

_a_ *Terminate* means   a. to end.   b. to revive.   c. to begin.

Matching Words with Definitions

Following are definitions of the ten words. Clearly write or print each word next to its definition. The sentences above and on the previous page will help you decide on the meaning of each word.

1. _elicit_ — To draw forth
2. _terminate_ — To stop; bring to an end
3. _methodical_ — Orderly; systematic
4. _adjacent_ — Close; near (to something)
5. _tangible_ — Able to be touched; having form and matter
6. _obsolete_ — No longer active or in use; out of date
7. _escalate_ — To increase or intensify
8. _acclaim_ — Great praise or applause; enthusiastic approval
9. _engross_ — To hold the full attention of; absorb
10. _exploit_ — To use selfishly or unethically; take unfair advantage of

CAUTION: Do not go any further until you are sure the above answers are correct. Then you can use the definitions to help you in the following practices. Your goal is eventually to know the words well enough so that you don't need to check the definitions at all.

➤ *Sentence Check 1*

Using the answer line provided, complete each item below with the correct word from the box. Use each word once.

a. **acclaim**	b. **adjacent**	c. **elicit**	d. **engross**	e. **escalate**
f. **exploit**	g. **methodical**	h. **obsolete**	i. **tangible**	j. **terminate**

_____ *tangible* _____   1. A wedding ring is a(n) ___ expression of a couple's commitment to each other.

_____ *obsolete* _____   2. If solar energy becomes as cheap and plentiful as sunshine, nuclear energy, which is expensive, may become ___.

_____ *acclaim* _____   3. Susan Sarandon's performance in *Dead Man Walking* won the actress an Oscar and the ___ of admiring critics.

_____ *adjacent* _____   4. Our house is ___ to one with a high wooden fence, so our view on that side is completely blocked.

_____ *escalate* _____   5. The shouting match between Rose and her brother ___(e)d until it was so loud that the neighbors complained.

_____ *engross* _____   6. Sometimes an article I'm reading on the bus will ___ me so much that I'll pass my stop.

_____ *exploit* _____   7. When workers feel ___(e)d by their employers, they often go on strike for larger salaries and better working conditions.

_____ *methodical* _____   8. Diana is very ___ about writing letters. She keeps her writing materials in one spot, makes a list of the people she owes letters to, and writes once a week.

_____ *terminate* _____   9. When Luke was caught stealing money on the job, the company ___(e)d his employment and brought him up on criminal charges.

_____ *elicit* _____   10. In one disturbing survey, the question "Which do you like better, TV or Daddy?"___(e)d this response from a number of children: "TV."

NOTE: Now check your answers to these questions by turning to page 127. Going over the answers carefully will help you prepare for the next two practices, for which answers are not given.

➤ *Sentence Check 2*

Using the answer lines provided, complete each item below with **two** words from the box. Use each word once.

_____ *engross* _____
_____ *elicit* _____   1–2. The gifted ice skater's routine ___(e)d the audience. It was the epitome° of grace and power combined. At the end, a long, rapid spin ___(e)d a burst of applause.

_____ *obsolete* _____
_____ *terminate* _____   3–4. Although hand-crafted furniture is almost ___, mass production hasn't yet___(e)d all demand for it.

_____ tangible _____   5–6. Workers want ___ rewards such as money and a pension, but they also
_____ acclaim _____   welcome less concrete benefits, such as ___ for a job well done.

_____ exploit _____   7–8. The more the British ___(e)d the American colonies by taxing them
_____ escalate _____   unfairly, the more the colonists' animosity° toward the British ___(e)d.

_____ methodical _____   9–10. Patty's ___ baking technique includes arranging all ingredients in a
_____ adjacent _____   row, with each one ___ to the one that is used after it.

➤ _Final Check:_ A Cruel Sport

Here is a final opportunity for you to strengthen your knowledge of the ten words. First read the following selection carefully. Then fill in each blank with a word from the box at the top of the previous page. (Context clues will help you figure out which word goes in which blank.) Use each word once.

The nightclub lights dimmed, and a spotlight revealed a short, fat man holding a heavy chain. He tugged the chain, and a muzzled bear appeared. The man, the animal's owner, announced that the bear's name was Sally. He would give a hundred dollars, he said, to anyone who wrestled Sally to the floor. Alex, sitting in the audience, was shocked. He had thought bear wrestling was (1)_____ obsolete _____, given up long ago as a cruel sport.

The offer (2)_____ elicit _____(e)d an eager response. "I'll do it!" one man called, winning the (3)_____ acclaim _____ of the spectators, who cheered him on. He went up and started to swing at Sally. She tried to back away. The match greatly (4)_____ engross _____(e)d most of the audience members, who watched every move. A stranger sitting (5)_____ adjacent _____ to Alex became so excited that he accidentally knocked over Alex's drink.

"Knock her on her rear!" the owner shouted. When Sally finally raised a paw to defend herself, her owner jerked her back with a sharp tug. Sally's antagonist° could then see that she had no claws. He thus felt more confident, so his attack (6)_____ escalate _____(e)d. But when the man fighting the bear seemed likely to pin Sally, her owner allowed the bear to throw him off. At that, the owner (7)_____ terminate _____(e)d the match, calling out "Next!"

Another man then sprang to his feet. And soon another. There were six more matches, each with the same result. It was clear to Alex that this show always followed the same (8)_____ methodical _____ routine.

Finally, the owner led Sally away. Her drooping head and labored walk were (9)_____ tangible _____ expressions of the animal's misery. Alex was more certain than ever that bear wrestling (10)_____ exploit _____(e)d the animal for human entertainment and that anyone who treated animals so cruelly was amoral°. As Sally passed his table, Alex heard her moaning softly. Looking closely, he saw that the bear was old, and completely blind.

Scores	Sentence Check 2 _____%	Final Check _____%

Enter your scores above and in the vocabulary performance chart on the inside back cover of the book.

allusion	banal
altruistic	euphemism
appease	mercenary
arbitrary	syndrome
assail	taint

Ten Words in Context

In the space provided, write the letter of the meaning closest to that of each **boldfaced** word. Use the context of the sentences to help you figure out each word's meaning.

1 **allusion**
(ə-lōō′zhən)
-noun

- After I suggested that Monty have fruit for dessert instead of chocolate cake, he responded, "Is that an **allusion** to my weight?"
- Ray didn't have the courage to come right out and ask Lucy to marry him. Instead, he made only an **allusion** to marriage by asking, "Wouldn't it be easier if we had to fill out just one tax return?"

_b_ *Allusion* means   a. a contrast.   b. a reference.   c. an answer.

2 **altruistic**
(ăl′trōō-ĭs′tĭk)
-adjective

- When an enemy approaches, ground squirrels show **altruistic** behavior. They risk their own lives to give alarm calls to nearby relatives.
- "I'm not often **altruistic**," Brett admitted. "I usually put my own welfare first."

_a_ *Altruistic* means   a. unselfish.   b. cheerful.   c. greedy.

3 **appease**
(ə-pēz′)
-verb

- My sister was so outraged when I accidentally scratched her favorite old Beatles record that nothing I could say or do would **appease** her.
- Roger was furious when he saw me out with another guy, but I quickly **appeased** him by explaining that the "date" was my cousin.

_c_ *Appease* means   a. to annoy.   b. to heal.   c. to calm.

4 **arbitrary**
(är′bĭ-trĕr′ē)
-adjective

- Professor Miller's students were angry that he graded essays in an **arbitrary** way, rather than using clear-cut standards.
- Parents should not enforce rules according to their moods. Such **arbitrary** discipline only confuses children.

_c_ *Arbitrary* means   a. steady.   b. slow.   c. impulsive.

5 **assail**
(ə-sāl′)
-verb

- The storm **assailed** us with hail and heavy rain.
- The two candidates continuously **assailed** each other with accusations of dishonesty.

_a_ *Assail* means   a. to attack.   b. to confuse.   c. to support.

6 **banal**
(bə-năl′)
-adjective

- The film, with its overused expressions and unimaginative plot, was the most **banal** I had ever seen.
- "Nice to see you" may be a **banal** comment, but what it lacks in originality it makes up for in friendliness.

_b_ *Banal* means   a. greedy.   b. unoriginal.   c. clever.

7 euphemism
(yōō′fə-mĭz′əm)
-noun

- Common **euphemisms** include "final resting place" (for *grave*), "intoxicated" (for *drunk*), and "powder room" (for *toilet*).
- The Central Intelligence Agency is on record as having referred to assassination with the **euphemism** "change of health."

_b_ *Euphemism* means   a. a harsh term.   b. a term that doesn't offend.   c. a foreign term.

8 mercenary
(mûr′sə-nĕr′ē)
-adjective

- Ed is totally **mercenary**. His philosophy is, "Pay me enough, and I'll do anything."
- The con man pretended to love the wealthy widow, but he actually married her for **mercenary** reasons.

_c_ *Mercenary* means   a. jealous.   b. angry.   c. greedy.

9 syndrome
(sĭn′drōm)
-noun

- Headaches are usually harmless, but as part of a **syndrome** including fever and a stiff neck, they may be a sign of a serious illness.
- Jet lag is a **syndrome** resulting from flying long distances; it often includes exhaustion, headache, and loss of appetite.

_a_ *Syndrome* means   a. a group of symptoms.   b. a cause.   c. something required.

10 taint
(tānt)
-verb

- The involvement of organized crime has **tainted** many sports, including boxing and horse racing.
- The government scandal **tainted** the reputations of everyone involved.

_b_ *Taint* means   a. to benefit.   b. to damage.   c. to start.

Matching Words with Definitions

Following are definitions of the ten words. Clearly write or print each word next to its definition. The sentences above and on the previous page will help you decide on the meaning of each word.

1. arbitrary — Determined by personal judgment, not rule or reason; based on impulse
2. mercenary — Motivated only by financial gain; greedy
3. allusion — An indirect reference
4. syndrome — A group of symptoms typical of a particular disease or condition
5. euphemism — A mild or vague term used as a substitute for one considered offensive or unpleasant
6. appease — To calm, especially by giving in to the demands of
7. banal — Lacking originality; overused; commonplace
8. taint — To stain the honor of someone or something
9. assail — To attack physically or verbally
10. altruistic — Unselfishly concerned for the welfare of others; unselfish

CAUTION: Do not go any further until you are sure the above answers are correct. Then you can use the definitions to help you in the following practices. Your goal is eventually to know the words well enough so that you don't need to check the definitions at all.

➤ *Sentence Check 1*

Using the answer line provided, complete each item below with the correct word from the box. Use each word once.

a. **allusion**	b. **altruistic**	c. **appease**	d. **arbitrary**	e. **assail**
f. **banal**	g. **euphemism**	h. **mercenary**	i. **syndrome**	j. **taint**

_____*mercenary*_____   1. There have been people ___ enough to sell their own children for the right price.

_____*allusion*_____   2. "Someone hasn't shown me his report card," my mother said, making a(n) ___ to my brother.

_____*altruistic*_____   3. It takes a(n) ___ person to adopt a disabled child.

_____*assail*_____   4. The mugger ___ed his victims with a baseball bat.

_____*euphemism*_____   5. The local undertaker insists on using a(n) ___ for the chapel of his funeral parlor. He calls it the "slumber room."

_____*taint*_____   6. The report that the halfback was addicted to drugs ___(e)d the team's image.

_____*appease*_____   7. The only thing that would ___ the dead boy's parents was imprisonment of the drunk driver who had killed him.

_____*syndrome*_____   8. Abraham Lincoln is thought to have had Marfan's ___, a group of symptoms which includes unusually long bones and abnormal blood circulation.

_____*arbitrary*_____   9. The judge's harsh sentence was ___. Rather than being based on past similar cases or on the seriousness of the crime, it was based on the judge's opinion of the defendant.

_____*banal*_____   10. "You're special" probably appears on thousands of greeting cards, but when someone says it to you and means it, it never seems ___.

NOTE: Now check your answers to these questions by turning to page 127. Going over the answers carefully will help you prepare for the next two practices, for which answers are not given.

➤ *Sentence Check 2*

Using the answer lines provided, complete each item below with **two** words from the box. Use each word once.

_____*Altruistic*_____
_____*mercenary*_____   1–2. ___ people tend to place the public welfare above their own self-interest. In contrast, ___ people will exploit° anyone for a profit—they will even sell harmful products.

_____*assail*_____
_____*appease*_____   3–4. The angry customer loudly ___(e)d the salesman for having sold her a broken clock. The salesman quickly ___(e)d her by giving her a full refund.

_____ *arbitrary* _____ 5–6. My boss judges performance in a(n) ___ manner, praising and scolding according to his moods. And when he says, "Please stay a few minutes longer today," "a few minutes" is a(n) ___ for "an hour."

_____ *euphemism* _____

_____ *syndrome* _____ 7–8. A certain rare ___ includes a very odd symptom—an uncontrollable urge to use obscene language. This disease can ___ a victim's reputation, because some people who hear the foul language won't understand the reason for it.

_____ *taint* _____

_____ *banal* _____ 9–10. The critic hated stale language. Instead of writing a(n) ___ comment such as "That ballerina is light on her feet," he made an interesting ___ to the dancer's movements: "She was never heavier than moonlight."

_____ *allusion* _____

➤ *Final Check:* No Luck with Women

Here is a final opportunity for you to strengthen your knowledge of the ten words. First read the following selection carefully. Then fill in each blank with a word from the box at the top of the previous page. (Context clues will help you figure out which word goes in which blank.) Use each word once.

I don't have much luck with women. The other night at a singles dance, I encountered° an attractive lady and asked her, "Excuse me, do you have the time?" (I admit the question is a bit (1)_____*banal*_____, but I couldn't think of anything more clever.) She replied, "Isn't that kind of personal?" Another woman got really upset just because I asked, "Haven't we met before, at Weight Watchers?" Okay, so I was wrong. I didn't mean to make a(n) (2)_____*allusion*_____ to her size. Still, after that, nothing I said would (3)_____*appease*_____ her.

Women don't appreciate how nice I am. First of all, I'm not particularly (4)_____*mercenary*_____. For instance, I've never considered a woman's wealth the most important thing about her. It's the second most important thing. And I would never (5)_____*taint*_____ a woman's reputation by letting her be seen with me in a decent place. I'm so (6)_____*altruistic*_____ that I once took care of a guy who was drunk by sending him home in a cab. Instead of being grateful, his attractive date (who had been in the ladies' room) (7)_____*assail*_____(e)d me with all sorts of accusations. How was I supposed to know she was his wife?

When I ask women out, they often answer me with (8)_____*euphemism*_____s such as "I already have plans" or "I'm busy." What they really mean is, "I'm busy making plans to avoid you." You'd think I suffer from some horrible, infectious (9)_____*syndrome*_____.

Women's behavior is totally (10)_____*arbitrary*_____. At least, I can't see any reason to it. Last night, for example, a woman I was nice enough to treat to a Coke threw it in my face. Thank goodness, she didn't get any on my day-glo Mickey Mouse tie.

| *Scores* | Sentence Check 2 _____ % | Final Check _____ % |

Enter your scores above and in the vocabulary performance chart on the inside back cover of the book.

CHAPTER

4

calamity	persevere
comprehensive	ponder
conventional	rehabilitate
flagrant	turmoil
fluctuate	venture

Ten Words in Context

In the space provided, write the letter of the meaning closest to that of each **boldfaced** word. Use the context of the sentences to help you figure out each word's meaning.

1 **calamity**
(kə-lăm′ĭ-tē)
-*noun*

- The survivors of the earthquake slowly rebuilt their homes and lives after the **calamity**.
- Our neighbor's house burned down one night in May. Ever since that **calamity**, our children have been afraid to go to bed at night.

_b_ *Calamity* means   a. an activity.   b. a tragedy.   c. a risk.

2 **comprehensive**
(kŏm′prē-hĕn′sĭv)
-*adjective*

- That article on sightseeing in New Orleans was not **comprehensive**. It failed to mention many points of interest in that wonderful city.
- Our company's **comprehensive** insurance plan covers most health services, including hospitals, doctors, and dentists.

_a_ *Comprehensive* means   a. complete.   b. familiar.   c. continuous.

3 **conventional**
(kən-vĕn′shə-nəl)
-*adjective*

- The **conventional** Valentine's Day gifts are roses and chocolates.
- Jorge wanted to propose to Elena in the **conventional** manner, so in the middle of a restaurant, he got down on his knees and asked, "Will you marry me?"

_c_ *Conventional* means   a. out-of-the-way.   b. useful.   c. usual.

4 **flagrant**
(flā′grənt)
-*adjective*

- The use of campaign funds for the congressman's private business was a **flagrant** violation of the law.
- In **flagrant** disregard of his parents' stated wishes, Art wore a T-shirt and jeans to their dinner party.

_a_ *Flagrant* means   a. obvious.   b. acceptable.   c. minor.

5 **fluctuate**
(flŭk′chōō-āt′)
-*verb*

- My weight used to **fluctuate** between 150 and 190 pounds. Now it's steady, at 170 pounds.
- Desert temperatures can **fluctuate** by as much as fifty degrees between daytime and nighttime.

_b_ *Fluctuate* means   a. to continue.   b. to vary.   c. to follow.

6 **persevere**
(pûr′sə′vîr)
-*verb*

- "I know you're tired," Jack said, "but we've got to **persevere** and get to the camp before the storm hits."
- It was not easy to attend English classes while working at two jobs, but Nina **persevered** until she could speak English well.

_c_ *Persevere* means   a. to surrender.   b. to hold back.   c. to keep going.

7 **ponder**
(pŏn′dər)
-*verb*

- Too often we don't take time to **ponder** the possible consequences of our actions.
- Over the years, Mr. Madigan rarely took time to **ponder** the meaning of life. Since his heart attack, however, he's thought a lot about what is important to him.

c *Ponder* means

    a. to wait for.   b. to ignore.   c. to think about.

8 **rehabilitate**
(rē′hə-bĭl′ə-tāt)
-*verb*

- Most prisons make little effort to **rehabilitate** inmates so that they can lead productive, wholesome lives after their release.
- My grandfather learned to walk, write, and speak again in a program that **rehabilitates** stroke victims.

b *Rehabilitate* means

    a. to pay back.   b. to prepare for normal life.   c. to depend upon.

9 **turmoil**
(tûr′moil)
-*noun*

- Without a teacher, the sixth-grade class was in **turmoil**, until the principal entered the room and the students quickly came to order.
- After the **turmoil** of crying babies, active children, and trying to feed 120 people, I'm glad when our family reunions end.

b *Turmoil* means

    a. discussion.   b. disorder.   c. harmony.

10 **venture**
(vĕn′chər)
-*verb*

- "I'll **venture** going on any ride in this amusement park except the Twister," said Nick. "I'll risk getting sick to my stomach, but I won't risk my life."
- At tomorrow's staff meeting, I will **venture** to say what I really think and cross my fingers that I don't get fired.

a *Venture* means

    a. to dare.   b. to remember.   c. to imagine.

Matching Words with Definitions

Following are definitions of the ten words. Clearly write or print each word next to its definition. The sentences above and on the previous page will help you decide on the meaning of each word.

1. _____*flagrant*_____   a. Shockingly obvious; outrageous

2. _____*venture*_____   b. To take the risk of; dare

3. _____*comprehensive*_____   c. Including all or much

4. _____*rehabilitate*_____   d. To restore to a normal life through therapy or education

5. _____*persevere*_____   e. To continue with an effort or plan despite difficulties

6. _____*turmoil*_____   f. Complete confusion; uproar

7. _____*calamity*_____   g. An event bringing great loss and misery

8. _____*fluctuate*_____   h. To vary irregularly; to go up and down or back and forth

9. _____*ponder*_____   i. To consider carefully; think deeply about

10. _____*conventional*_____   j. Customary; ordinary

CAUTION: Do not go any further until you are sure the above answers are correct. Then you can use the definitions to help you in the following practices. Your goal is eventually to know the words well enough so that you don't need to check the definitions at all.

➤ *Sentence Check 1*

Using the answer line provided, complete each item below with the correct word from the box. Use each word once.

| a. **calamity** | b. **comprehensive** | c. **conventional** | d. **flagrant** | e. **fluctuate** |
| f. **persevere** | g. **ponder** | h. **rehabilitate** | i. **turmoil** | j. **venture** |

calamity   1. Iris is so vain that she considers it a ___ if a pimple appears anywhere on her face.

ponder   2. Too many people have a child without taking time to ___ parenthood. They give less thought to having a baby than to buying a sofa.

flagrant   3. When Charlene lost her job because she spoke up for a fellow employee, it was a ___ violation of her rights.

comprehensive   4. Our psychology exam will be ___; it will cover everything we've studied since September.

conventional   5. Nobody in Doug's family has a ___ job. His mother is a drummer, his father is a magician, and his uncle is a wine taster.

persevere   6. Learning the computer program was difficult, but when Maria saw how useful it would be in her work, she was glad she had ___(e)d.

rehabilitate   7. It took many months of therapy to ___ my aunt after she lost her sight, but now she can get around her home and neighborhood on her own.

turmoil   8. The day we moved, the apartment was in ___. Boxes and people were everywhere, and the baby wouldn't stop crying.

fluctuate   9. The way my dog's appetite ___(e)d this week worries me. One day she hardly ate anything, and the next she gulped down everything I gave her.

venture   10. Instead of hiring a lawyer, the defendant will ___ to plead her own case in court.

NOTE: Now check your answers to these questions by turning to page 127. Going over the answers carefully will help you prepare for the next two practices, for which answers are not given.

➤ *Sentence Check 2*

Using the answer lines provided, complete each item below with **two** words from the box. Use each word once.

venture
calamity   1–2. The one time my cousin ___(e)d skydiving, the result was a ___. Her parachute didn't open, and she was injured so badly in the fall that she almost died.

rehabilitate
persevere   3–4. A drug-treatment center can ___ most addicts. Among the failures are addicts who don't ___ with the treatment and leave the center early.

conventional

flagrant

5–6. When driving alone, Marshall is very ___, obeying all the traffic rules. But when his friends are with him, he shows off with ___ violations of the speed limit.

ponder

comprehensive

7–8. "We need to ___ all we might do to help families in trouble," said the social worker to her staff. "We must plan a ___ program, not just a narrow plan dealing with only one part of their lives."

fluctuate

turmoil

9–10. Our boss's moods and orders ___ so wildly at times that they throw our department into ___. As a result of his arbitrary° behavior, our productivity is at an all-time low.

➤ _Final Check:_ Accident and Recovery

Here is a final opportunity for you to strengthen your knowledge of the ten words. First read the following selection carefully. Then fill in each blank with a word from the box at the top of the previous page. (Context clues will help you figure out which word goes in which blank.) Use each word once.

We tried to stop Anna from jumping, but her (1)_____ _flagrant_ _____ disregard of our warnings led to a (2)_____ _calamity_ _____ that would change her life forever. She dove off a rock into a river none of us was sure was deep enough. When she hit the bottom, she broke her back.

I visited Anna at the hospital every day for the next few weeks. I saw her mood (3)_____ _fluctuate_ _____ between anger and quiet depression. Her whole life seemed in (4)_____ _turmoil_ _____; she was too confused and unhappy to think reasonably about her future. Although I tried to cheer her up, nothing I said or did could appease° her.

Within about a month, however, I began to see a change in Anna. She had moved to Henner House to participate in a very (5)_____ _comprehensive_ _____ program, designed to meet all the needs of patients like Anna. The program (6)_____ _rehabilitate_ _____s accident victims so that they can return to fulfilling lives. Anna gained hope once she saw she could learn to do such everyday tasks as cooking, cleaning, and bathing. After learning how to get around indoors, she (7)_____ _venture_ _____(e)d traveling around the city in her wheelchair. The more she did, the better she felt. The staff also helped Anna plan for her future. They urged her to (8)_____ _ponder_ _____ her goals and how she might meet them. At times, it was difficult for her to (9)_____ _persevere_ _____ with the program, but she didn't quit.

Now, ten months later, Anna is able to live a somewhat (10)_____ _conventional_ _____ life. Despite her condition, she is able to do many of the ordinary things she used to do—work, drive, and live in an apartment with a friend. Yes, her life has changed forever. But Anna is once again glad to be alive.

Scores	Sentence Check 2 _____%	Final Check _____%

Enter your scores above and in the vocabulary performance chart on the inside back cover of the book.

attest	enigma
attribute	exemplify
discern	mobile
dispatch	nocturnal
enhance	orient

Ten Words in Context

In the space provided, write the letter of the meaning closest to that of each **boldfaced** word. Use the context of the sentences to help you figure out each word's meaning.

1 **attest**
(ə-tĕst′)
-verb

- Anyone who has seen the Golden Gate Bridge in the rose-gold light of sunset can **attest** to its beauty.
- Witnesses **attest** to the fact that rainfall makes the ground of Death Valley so slippery that boulders slide across it.

_a_ *Attest to* means
    a. to declare to be true.   b. to wish for.   c. to forget easily.

2 **attribute**
(ăt′rə-byōot′)
-noun

- A three-hundred-page novel written in 1939 has the odd **attribute** of containing no *e*, the most common letter in English.
- In Japan, some cars have such computerized **attributes** as windshield wipers that automatically turn on when it rains.

_c_ *Attribute* means
    a. a tendency.   b. a defect.   c. a characteristic.

3 **discern**
(dĭ-sûrn′)
-verb

- An experienced jeweler can easily **discern** whether a diamond is genuine or fake.
- People who are red-green colorblind can **discern** the colors of traffic lights by recognizing shades of gray.

_a_ *Discern* means
    a. to see clearly.   b. to disregard.   c. to change.

4 **dispatch**
(dĭ-spăch′)
-verb

- I wanted to **dispatch** the letter as quickly as possible, so I took it to the post office instead of dropping it into a mailbox.
- At work Harold is treated like an errand boy. His boss often **dispatches** him to the deli for sandwiches or donuts.

_b_ *Dispatch* means
    a. to represent.   b. to send.   c. to drive.

5 **enhance**
(ĕn-hăns′)
-verb

- Our gym teacher **enhanced** her appearance with a more attractive hairstyle.
- The college catalogue stated that the writing course would "**enhance** all students' writing skills" by improving their grammar and style.

_a_ *Enhance* means
    a. to improve.   b. to recognize.   c. to reduce.

6 **enigma**
(ĭ-nĭg′mə)
-noun

- How the thief entered our house was an **enigma** until we remembered that the cellar door had been left unlocked.
- The "singing sands" of Scotland remained an **enigma** until scientists learned that footsteps caused the round grains of sand and the surrounding air pockets to make musical vibrations.

_b_ *Enigma* means
    a. a comfort.   b. a puzzle.   c. an error.

7 **exemplify**
(ĭg-zĕm′plə-fī′)
-verb

- The many IRS employees who give citizens inaccurate information **exemplify** governmental incompetence.
- Mr. Pell, who emphasizes original thinking and freedom of expression, **exemplifies** the best in teaching.

_a_ *Exemplify* means   a. to illustrate.   b. to save.   c. to oppose.

8 **mobile**
(mō′bəl)
-adjective

- My parents own a **mobile** home, which can be moved from place to place on a long truck.
- Every morning when I was in the hospital, a volunteer wheeled a **mobile** library into my room.

_c_ *Mobile* means   a. active.   b. expensive.   c. movable.

9 **nocturnal**
(nŏk-tûr′nəl)
-adjective

- I know when my brother has enjoyed one of his **nocturnal** feasts because I find a stack of dishes in the sink in the morning.
- Being **nocturnal**, owls are rarely seen during the day.

_c_ *Nocturnal* means   a. noisy.   b. busy.   c. of the night.

10 **orient**
(ôr′ē-ĕnt)
-verb

- When coming up from the subway, I often need to look at a street sign to **orient** myself.
- Drivers of the future may **orient** themselves in unfamiliar places with the help of an electronic map that shows the car's location.

_a_ *Orient* means   a. to locate.   b. to welcome.   c. to question.

Matching Words with Definitions

Following are definitions of the ten words. Clearly write or print each word next to its definition. The sentences above and on the previous page will help you decide on the meaning of each word.

1. _____enigma_____   a. A mystery or puzzle

2. _____dispatch_____   b. To send to a specific place or on specific business

3. _____nocturnal_____   c. Of, about, or happening in the night; active at night

4. _____attest_____   d. To make a statement about something on the basis of personal experience; bear witness; testify

5. _____orient_____   e. To determine one's location or direction; to locate in relation to a direction (east, west, etc.)

6. _____discern_____   f. To recognize; detect

7. _____enhance_____   g. To improve

8. _____mobile_____   h. Moving or able to move from place to place

9. _____attribute_____   i. A quality or feature of a person or thing

10. _____exemplify_____   j. To be an example of; represent; be typical of

CAUTION: Do not go any further until you are sure the above answers are correct. Then you can use the definitions to help you in the following practices. Your goal is eventually to know the words well enough so that you don't need to check the definitions at all.

➤ *Sentence Check 1*

Using the answer line provided, complete each item below with the correct word from the box. Use each word once.

a. **attest**	b. **attribute**	c. **discern**	d. **dispatch**	e. **enhance**
f. **enigma**	g. **exemplify**	h. **mobile**	i. **nocturnal**	j. **orient**

_____*enhance*_____ 1. Fresh garlic may not ___ the breath, but it certainly improves spaghetti sauce.

_____*attest*_____ 2. A witness ___(e)d to the truth of the defendant's claim that she had loved the murdered man.

_____*dispatch*_____ 3. When I was younger, my mother used to ___ me to the store for milk or some missing cooking ingredient as often as twice a day.

_____*exemplify*_____ 4. The lives of such reformers as Susan B. Anthony, Gandhi, and Martin Luther King ___ greatness.

_____*enigma*_____ 5. Science does not have enough evidence to solve the ___ of whether or not there is other intelligent life in the universe.

_____*nocturnal*_____ 6. The convicts decided on a(n) ___ escape. The darkness would hide them as they fled through the forest.

_____*discern*_____ 7. Sue's hairpiece is so natural looking that it's impossible to ___ where the hairpiece ends and her own hair begins.

_____*orient*_____ 8. The positions of the stars help sailors ___ themselves on the open seas.

_____*mobile*_____ 9. My mother is unable to walk, but with her wheelchair she is ___ enough to get around her one-story home, move along a sidewalk, and even shop at a mall.

_____*attribute*_____ 10. Giant kelp, a form of seaweed, has some amazing ___s. Not only is it the world's fastest-growing vegetable, but the more it is cut, the faster it grows.

NOTE: Now check your answers to these questions by turning to page 127. Going over the answers carefully will help you prepare for the next two practices, for which answers are not given.

➤ *Sentence Check 2*

Using the answer lines provided, complete each item below with **two** words from the box. Use each word once.

_____*enhance*_____
_____*discern*_____ 1–2. Because Helen Keller could not hear or see, the keenness of her other senses was ___(e)d by use. It is said that she could ___ who was in a room simply by using her sense of smell.

_____*mobile*_____
_____*orient*_____ 3–4. A ___ robot that collects and delivers mail throughout our office building ___s itself with electric eyes.

_____ attribute _____   5–6. In fables, animals often illustrate human ___s. In the story of the race
_____ exemplify _____   between the tortoise and the hare, the tortoise is meant to ___ the human
                                  quality of being slow but steady. Despite competing against a much
                                  speedier antagonist°, he persevered° and beat the overly confident hare.

_____ dispatch _____   7–8. The reason the boss likes to ___ Oliver on lengthy errands is no ___.
_____ enigma _____   Everyone knows that the office functions better with Oliver out of the
                                  way.

_____ attest _____   9–10. Anyone who has ever gone to college can ___ to the fact that, during
_____ nocturnal _____   finals, many students become ___ animals. They stay up all night before
                                   an exam and then sleep during the daytime after taking the test.

➤ _Final Check:_ Animal Senses

Here is a final opportunity for you to strengthen your knowledge of the ten words. First read the following selection carefully. Then fill in each blank with a word from the box at the top of the previous page. (Context clues will help you figure out which word goes in which blank.) Use each word once.

Animals possess sensory powers that humans lack. Homing pigeons fly with great speed and accuracy when (1)_____ dispatch _____(e)d with messages to faraway places. How do pigeons (2)_____ orient _____ themselves in unfamiliar regions? This remains something of a(n) (3)_____ enigma _____. The mystery, however, is partly explained by a pigeon's ability to see ultraviolet light, which reveals the sun's position even through clouds. In addition, pigeons can hear sound waves that have traveled hundreds of miles. These waves (4)_____ enhance _____ a pigeon's sense of direction by indicating distant mountains and seas. Pigeons even appear to (5)_____ discern _____ changes in the earth's magnetic field.

Bats have impressive (6)_____ attribute _____s equally worthy of acclaim°. As (7)_____ nocturnal _____ animals, they search for food in complete darkness. They do so by screeching in tones higher than any human can hear and then locating prey by the returning echoes.

Scorpions also (8)_____ exemplify _____ the night hunter. Tiny leg hairs enable them to feel vibrations in the sand made by a (9)_____ mobile _____ insect as far as two feet away.

People with knowledge of the pigeon, bat, and scorpion can (10)_____ attest _____ to the fact that such "inventions" as the magnetic compass, radar, and the motion detector are nothing new.

Scores Sentence Check 2 _____%	Final Check _____%

Enter your scores above and in the vocabulary performance chart on the inside back cover of the book.

UNIT ONE: Review

The box at the right lists twenty-five words from Unit One. Using the clues at the bottom of the page, fill in these words to complete the puzzle that follows.

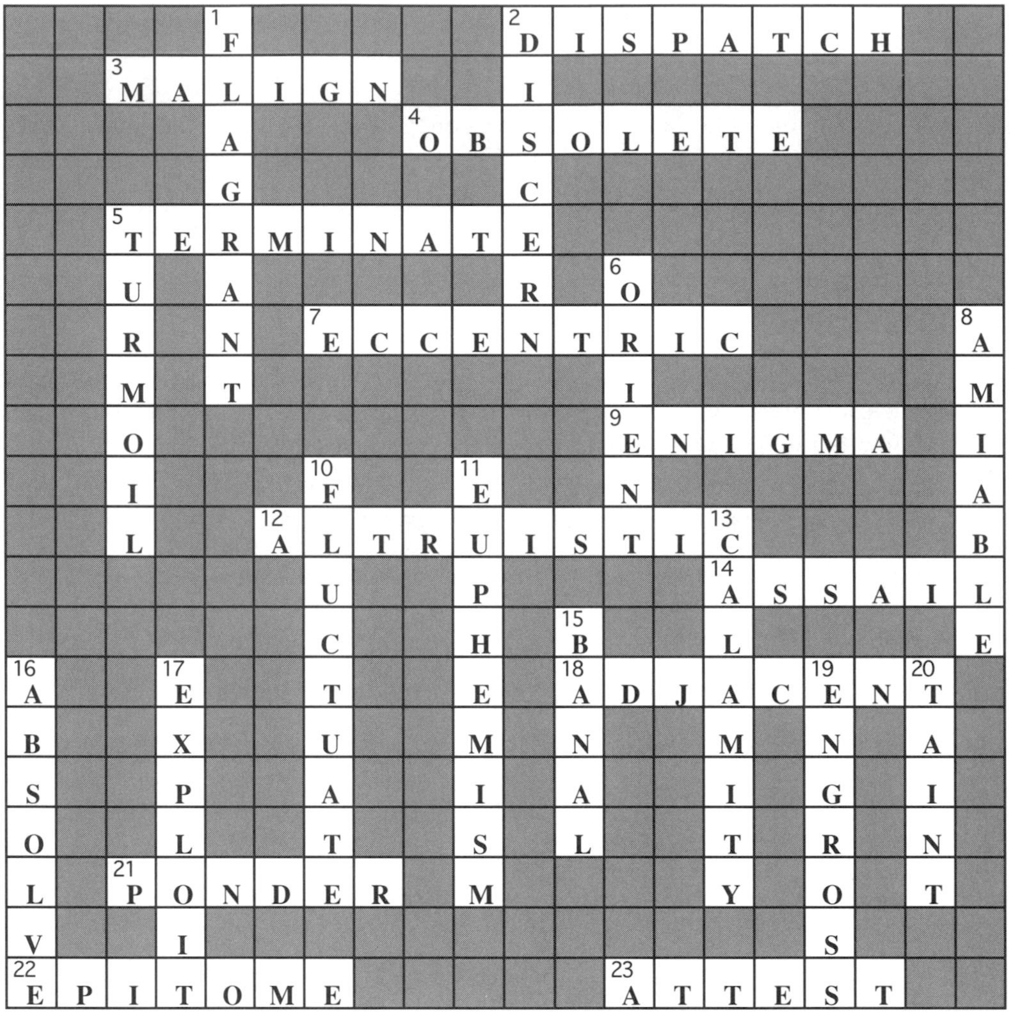

The crossword grid contains the following filled answers:

- 2 ACROSS: DISPATCH
- 3 ACROSS: MALIGN
- 4 ACROSS: OBSOLETE
- 5 ACROSS: TERMINATE
- 7 ACROSS: ECCENTRIC
- 9 ACROSS: ENIGMA
- 12 ACROSS: ALTRUISTIC
- 14 ACROSS: ASSAIL
- 18 ACROSS: ADJACENT
- 21 ACROSS: PONDER
- 22 ACROSS: EPITOME
- 23 ACROSS: ATTEST

Down answers include: FLAGRANT, MALIGN, DISCERN, TURMOIL, RAMANT, ORIENT, AMIABLE, FLUCTUATE, EUPHEMISM, ENGROSS, CALAMITY, BANAL, ABSOLVE, EXPLOIT, TAINT

Word box:

absolve
adjacent
altruistic
amiable
assail
attest
banal
calamity
discern
dispatch
eccentric
engross
enigma
epitome
euphemism
exploit
flagrant
fluctuate
malign
obsolete
orient
ponder
taint
terminate
turmoil

ACROSS

2. To send to a specific place or on specific business
3. To make evil and often untrue statements about; speak evil of
4. No longer active in use; out of date
5. To stop; bring to an end
7. Differing from what is customary; odd
9. A mystery or puzzle
12. Unselfishly concerned for the welfare of others; unselfish
14. To attack physically or verbally
18. Close; near (to something)
21. To consider carefully; think deeply about
22. A perfect or typical example of a general quality or type
23. To make a statement about something on the basis of personal experience; bear witness; testify

DOWN

1. Shockingly obvious; outrageous
2. To recognize; detect
5. Complete confusion; uproar
6. To determine one's location or direction; to locate in relation to a direction
8. Good-natured; friendly
10. To vary irregularly; to go up and down or back and forth
11. A mild or vague term used as a substitute for one that is offensive or unpleasant
13. An event bringing great loss or misery
15. Lacking originality; overused; commonplace
16. To find innocent or blameless
17. To use selfishly or unethically; take unfair advantage of
19. To hold the full attention of
20. To stain the honor of someone or something

UNIT ONE: Test 1

PART A
Choose the word that best completes each item and write it in the space provided.

_____euphemism_____ 1. A common ___ for *corpse* is "remains."

    a. acclaim   b. attribute   c. euphemism   d. turmoil

_____rehabilitate_____ 2. The counseling program to ___ addicts includes job training.

    a. rehabilitate   b. attest   c. ponder   d. exemplify

_____nocturnal_____ 3. According to legend, vampires are ___ creatures who cannot survive in daylight.

    a. altruistic   b. banal   c. nocturnal   d. obsolete

_____escalates_____ 4. In the winter, the price of tomatoes ___ while their quality goes down.

    a. elicits   b. appeases   c. escalates   d. absolves

_____mercenary_____ 5. The taxi driver was so ___ that he charged his own mother for a ride.

    a. mercenary   b. arbitrary   c. mobile   d. obsolete

_____obsolete_____ 6. You probably thought that mail delivery by mule was ___, but it still exists in the Grand Canyon.

    a. adamant   b. mercenary   c. tangible   d. obsolete

_____altruistic_____ 7. So ___ that he refused to take money from the public for his discovery of x-rays, Wilhelm Roentgen died poor.

    a. nocturnal   b. altruistic   c. amoral   d. comprehensive

_____calamity_____ 8. The sinking of the ship *Titanic*, which struck an iceberg, was a(n) ___ in which nearly 1,600 people died.

    a. allusion   b. animosity   c. calamity   d. attribute

_____acclaim_____ 9. Although Marilyn Monroe received great ___ from adoring fans and critics, she never received an Oscar.

    a. animosity   b. calamity   c. turmoil   d. acclaim

_____absolved_____ 10. The model realized that if she wanted to be ___ of the charges, she'd better hire a detective to find the real murderer.

    a. assailed   b. enhanced   c. pondered   d. absolved

(Continues on next page)

_____*epitome*_____ 11. The ___ of refreshment is drinking an ice-cold lemonade on a sizzling hot day.

   a. taint   b. epitome   c. animosity   d. syndrome

_____*dispatch*_____ 12. The Peace Corps continues to ___ American volunteers to live and work in developing nations.

   a. discern   b. appease   c. dispatch   d. fluctuate

PART B
Write **C** if the italicized word is used **correctly**. Write **I** if the word is used **incorrectly**.

_C_ 13. It's hard to *discern* the differences between the Fields twins.

_I_ 14. The Olympic swimmer *pondered* across the pool in record time.

_I_ 15. The man *attested* to his crime, pleading not guilty to all charges.

_I_ 16. Every day, people *enhance* the tropical rainforests by destroying some twenty thousand acres.

_C_ 17. Students often *exploit* the presence of a substitute teacher by using fake names.

_C_ 18. It's healthier to stay the same weight than to *fluctuate* up and down.

_I_ 19. The passerby showed his *animosity* by entering the burning house and pulling the child to safety.

_I_ 20. If you worry about the environment, you're *eccentric*. According to a poll, over three-fourths of Americans are concerned about the environment.

_C_ 21. In 1876, Wild Bill Hickok was in a poker game that was *terminated* by a bullet entering the back of his head.

_C_ 22. A wedding ring is a *tangible* expression of a couple's commitment to each other.

_C_ 23. Phyllis is very *methodical* in her efforts to be the life of any party. She keeps a file box of jokes, indexed by occasion.

_C_ 24. The symptoms of fetal alcohol *syndrome* include deformed limbs and mental retardation.

_I_ 25. Our *amiable* neighbor scares our children so much that they refuse to knock on his door even on Halloween.

Score (Number correct) _____ x 4 = _____ %

Enter your score above and in the vocabulary performance chart on the inside back cover of the book.

UNIT ONE: Test 2

PART A
Complete each item with a word from the box. Use each word once.

a. **adamant**	b. **allusion**	c. **amoral**	d. **antagonist**
e. **appease**	f. **attribute**	g. **comprehensive**	h. **elicit**
i. **enigma**	j. **flagrant**	k. **orient**	l. **persevere**

_____persevere_____ 1. Marathon runners must ___ beyond the point at which they start to feel pain.

_____orient_____ 2. People who can't read must ___ themselves in a city by relating to familiar places, not signs.

_____attribute_____ 3. In some religions, gods and goddesses represent various human ___s, such as strength, beauty, and wisdom.

_____antagonist_____ 4. The ___s in the debate took opposing sides on the question of outlawing cigarettes.

_____elicit_____ 5. Apparently, the chance to be President doesn't ___ much enthusiasm from most Americans—89 percent say they wouldn't want the job.

_____amoral_____ 6. It's often said that nature is ___. However, humans are part of nature, and most of them *do* have a moral sense.

_____comprehensive_____ 7. To get a bachelor's degree from some universities, students must take a(n) ___ exam that tests their overall knowledge of their major field.

_____adamant_____ 8. Our congressional representative, ___ in her opposition to pesticides, often reminds voters that pesticides kill about fourteen thousand people each year.

_____allusion_____ 9. "Gail isn't the only athlete in the family," Clarence said, making a(n) ___ to Gail's father, a bowling champion.

_____appease_____ 10. When Kathleen stood Evan up for the prom, an apology did not ___ him. He's suing her for the cost of his rented tux and the prom tickets.

_____flagrant_____ 11. In a race across New Jersey in 1901, drivers traveling up to thirty miles an hour were arrested for their ___ disregard of the speed limit, which was eight miles an hour.

_____enigma_____ 12. The thousands of oak leaves that covered the ground in a Scottish town in 1889 were a(n) ___. The nearest oak trees were eight miles away.

(Continues on next page)

PART B
Write **C** if the italicized word is used **correctly**. Write **I** if the word is used **incorrectly**.

_I_ 13. Cory was so *engrossed* in the film that he fell asleep.

_I_ 14. The *turmoil* of a smooth, clear lake always makes me feel at peace.

_C_ 15. Our veterinarian has a *mobile* office, a fully equipped van which she drives to patients' homes.

_C_ 16. In my dreams, I *venture* to perform feats that I would never dare when awake, such as leaping from roof to roof along a row of houses.

_C_ 17. When, during our drive, we *encountered* an unexpected hailstorm, we felt as if we were inside a metal can being pelted with stones.

_I_ 18. The critic *maligned* the folk singer by saying her voice has both richness and sparkle, like velvet trimmed with gold.

_I_ 19. In 1971, three dolphins *assailed* a drowning woman by keeping her afloat and protecting her from sharks across two hundred miles of ocean.

_C_ 20. When the evidence in a case is unclear, a jury's decision may be *arbitrary*, based on only the jurors' "gut feeling."

_I_ 21. Alice Walker's novel *The Color Purple* won both the Pulitzer Prize and the National Book Award because critics found her writing so *banal*.

_C_ 22. Lightning bolts, which travel at millions of miles an hour and produce five times the heat of the sun's surface, *exemplify* nature's tremendous energy.

_C_ 23. We had to trim the oak tree *adjacent* to our house so that its branches wouldn't reach into the porch.

_I_ 24. Before leaving for Antarctica, a team of explorers packed such *conventional* equipment as twenty hula hoops.

_C_ 25. Eager to *taint* his opponent's reputation, the candidate spent thousands of dollars on research aimed at uncovering some scandal.

| *Score* (Number correct) _____ x 4 = _____ % |

UNIT ONE: *Test 3*

PART A: Synonyms
In the space provided, write the letter of the choice that is most nearly the **same** in meaning as the **boldfaced** word.

_d_	1. **tangible**	a) movable	b) spiritual	c) calm	d) touchable
_c_	2. **calamity**	a) invention	b) anger	c) tragedy	d) event
_a_	3. **attest**	a) testify	b) teach	c) respond	d) stain
_c_	4. **elicit**	a) state	b) attack	c) draw out	d) avoid
_b_	5. **allusion**	a) problem	b) reference	c) behavior	d) insult
_b_	6. **fluctuate**	a) lean	b) vary	c) prevent	d) stand still
_a_	7. **encounter**	a) meet	b) buy	c) continue despite difficulties	d) depend
_b_	8. **ponder**	a) recognize	b) think over	c) use	d) refuse
_d_	9. **arbitrary**	a) illegal	b) governed by law	c) odd	d) based on impulse
_c_	10. **exemplify**	a) praise	b) excuse	c) illustrate	d) send for
_b_	11. **obsolete**	a) personal	b) old-fashioned	c) noisy	d) commonplace
_a_	12. **antagonist**	a) opponent	b) supporter	c) question	d) response
_b_	13. **exploit**	a) assist	b) abuse	c) leave	d) increase
_d_	14. **euphemism**	a) quotation	b) main point	c) trait	d) inoffensive term
_d_	15. **orient**	a) consider carefully	b) please	c) continue	d) locate
_b_	16. **appease**	a) end	b) calm down	c) take advantage of	d) begin
_a_	17. **discern**	a) see	b) forget	c) interest	d) deny
_c_	18. **rehabilitate**	a) repeat	b) come upon	c) restore to normality	d) clear of guilt
_b_	19. **attribute**	a) confusion	b) characteristic	c) regret	d) ill will
_a_	20. **venture**	a) dare	b) increase	c) improve	d) intrude on
_a_	21. **epitome**	a) perfect model	b) puzzle	c) goal	d) exception
_c_	22. **syndrome**	a) confusion	b) reference	c) typical symptoms	d) main point
_c_	23. **flagrant**	a) unlikely	b) out of date	c) outrageous	d) true
_d_	24. **dispatch**	a) vary	b) repair	c) show	d) send
_a_	25. **enigma**	a) riddle	b) example	c) term	d) disaster

(Continues on next page)

PART B: Antonyms
In the space provided, write the letter of the choice that is most nearly the **opposite** in meaning to the **boldfaced** word.

_d_ 26. **nocturnal**   a) early   b) late   c) normal   **d)** by day

_b_ 27. **altruistic**   a) unfriendly   **b)** selfish   c) usual   d) not well-known

_c_ 28. **comprehensive** a) interesting   b) puzzling   **c)** limited   d) obvious

_d_ 29. **assail**   a) avoid   b) continue   c) stop   **d)** defend

_b_ 30. **enhance**   a) prove   **b)** worsen   c) support   d) resist

_c_ 31. **acclaim**   a) statement   b) recognition   **c)** criticism   d) assistance

_a_ 32. **banal**   **a)** original   b) old   c) orderly   d) unselfish

_c_ 33. **amoral**   a) dependable   b) calm   **c)** ethical   d) based on personal choice

_b_ 34. **mobile**   a) medical   **b)** immovable   c) harmful   d) cautious

_a_ 35. **absolve**   **a)** blame   b) solve   c) bring to a state of peace   d) annoy

_c_ 36. **eccentric**   a) nearby   b) generous   **c)** ordinary   d) disorganized

_d_ 37. **persevere**   a) build   b) add to   c) blame   **d)** quit

_d_ 38. **animosity**   a) spirituality   b) beauty   c) opposition   **d)** friendliness

_b_ 39. **engross**   a) delight   **b)** bore   c) make active   d) discourage

_d_ 40. **adamant**   a) straightforward   b) greedy   c) enormous   **d)** flexible

_a_ 41. **escalate**   **a)** lessen   b) lift   c) cause   d) form an opinion

_c_ 42. **mercenary**   a) rich   b) unusual   **c)** generous   d) careless

_a_ 43. **terminate**   **a)** begin   b) study   c) pay attention to   d) compete

_b_ 44. **malign**   a) recover   **b)** praise   c) be consistent   d) move

_b_ 45. **turmoil**   a) admiration   **b)** peace and quiet   c) blessing   d) reality

_b_ 46. **amiable**   a) nearby   **b)** disagreeable   c) athletic   d) unusual

_b_ 47. **adjacent**   a) unfamiliar   **b)** distant   c) ordinary   d) unclear

_d_ 48. **methodical**   a) clear   b) late   c) generous   **d)** disorganized

_a_ 49. **taint**   **a)** honor   b) delay   c) surprise   d) interfere

_b_ 50. **conventional**   a) lonely   **b)** uncommon   c) inconvenient   d) noticeable

Score (Number correct) _____ x 2 = _____ %

Enter your score above and in the vocabulary performance chart on the inside back cover of the book.

UNIT ONE: Test 4

PART A
Complete each sentence in a way that clearly shows you understand the meaning of the **boldfaced** word. Take a minute to plan your answer before you write.

Example: Being **nocturnal** animals, raccoons _____ *raid our garbage cans only at night* _____.

1. The news reported a **calamity** in which _____ *(Answers will vary.)* _____

   _____.

2. Typewriters are now almost **obsolete** because _____

   _____.

3. Three personal **attributes** that I possess are _____

   _____.

4. One **tangible** symbol of affection is _____

   _____.

5. When I take a bath, I often **ponder** _____

   _____.

6. The **eccentric** teacher has a habit of _____

   _____.

7. One advantage of a **mobile** library might be _____

   _____.

8. The most **altruistic** thing I ever saw anyone do was to _____

   _____.

9. The actor received this **acclaim** for his performance: "_____

   _____."

10. I plan to **persevere** in _____

    _____.

(Continues on next page)

PART B

After each **boldfaced** word are a *synonym* (a word that means the same as the boldfaced word), an *antonym* (a word that means the opposite of the boldfaced word), and a word that is neither. On the first answer line, write the letter of the word that is the synonym. On the second answer line, write the letter of the word that is the antonym.

Example: _a_ _c_ enhance   a. improve   b. lead   c. weaken

_c_ _b_ 11–12. **persevere**   a. look   b. stop   c. persist

_b_ _a_ 13–14. **comprehensive**   a. limited   b. broad   c. irregular

_a_ _b_ 15–16. **terminate**   a. end   b. begin   c. grow

_c_ _a_ 17–18. **amoral**   a. ethical   b. costly   c. unprincipled

_b_ _c_ 19–20. **assail**   a. flow   b. attack   c. defend

PART C

Use five of the following ten words in sentences. Make it clear that you know the meaning of the word you use. Feel free to use the past tense or plural form of a word.

a. **absolve**	b. **animosity**	c. **antagonist**	d. **appease**	e. **banal**
f. **encounter**	g. **engross**	h. **euphemism**	i. **mercenary**	j. **turmoil**

21. _____ *(Answers will vary.)* _____

_____

22. _____

_____

23. _____

_____

24. _____

_____

25. _____

_____

Score (Number correct) _____ x 4 = _____%

Enter your score above and in the vocabulary performance chart on the inside back cover of the book.

Unit Two

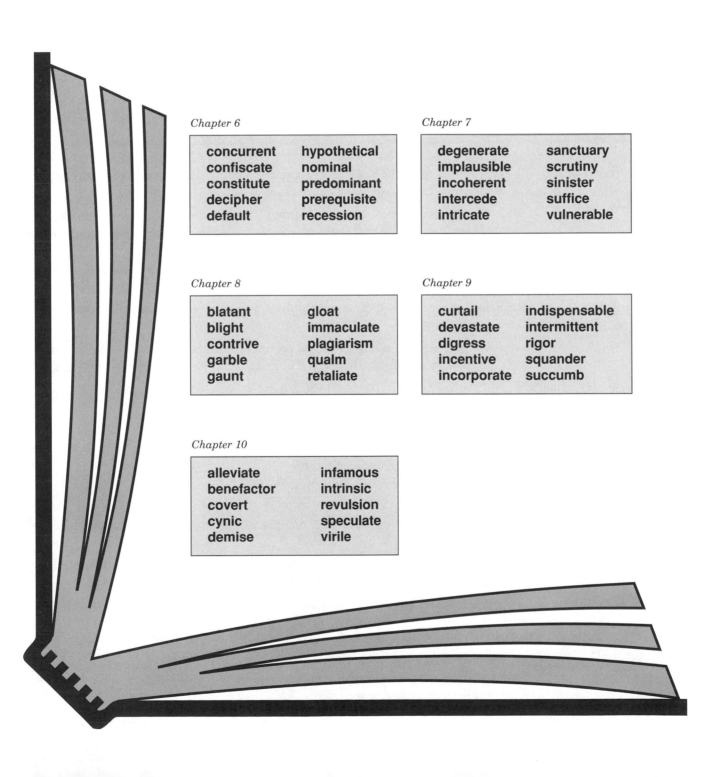

Chapter 6

concurrent	hypothetical
confiscate	nominal
constitute	predominant
decipher	prerequisite
default	recession

Chapter 7

degenerate	sanctuary
implausible	scrutiny
incoherent	sinister
intercede	suffice
intricate	vulnerable

Chapter 8

blatant	gloat
blight	immaculate
contrive	plagiarism
garble	qualm
gaunt	retaliate

Chapter 9

curtail	indispensable
devastate	intermittent
digress	rigor
incentive	squander
incorporate	succumb

Chapter 10

alleviate	infamous
benefactor	intrinsic
covert	revulsion
cynic	speculate
demise	virile

concurrent	hypothetical
confiscate	nominal
constitute	predominant
decipher	prerequisite
default	recession

Ten Words in Context

In the space provided, write the letter of the meaning closest to that of each **boldfaced** word. Use the context of the sentences to help you figure out each word's meaning.

1 **concurrent**
(kən-kûr′ənt)
-*adjective*

- Having mistakenly registered for two **concurrent** classes, Joe had to drop one of them and choose a course that met at a different time.
- **Concurrent** with the closing of the steel mill was the opening of a new toy factory in town. As a result, most of the workers laid off from the mill found jobs at the new factory.

a *Concurrent* means   a. occurring at the same time.   b. resulting.   c. noticeable.

2 **confiscate**
(kŏn′fĭs-kāt′)
-*verb*

- Not only did the teacher **confiscate** the note I passed to my boyfriend, but she also read it out loud to the entire class.
- Chinese drug agents once **confiscated** $2 million worth of heroin that had been wrapped in plastic and inserted into live goldfish. The agents seized the drugs as they were being sent out of the country.

b *Confiscate* means   a. to distribute widely.   b. to take possession of.   c. to overlook.

3 **constitute**
(kŏn′stĭ-tōot)
-*verb*

- In my opinion, a good movie, a pizza, and animated conversation **constitute** a perfect night out.
- Twelve business and professional people **constitute** the board of directors of the local women's shelter. Among other things, they help raise funds for the shelter.

c *Constitute* means   a. to repeat.   b. to oppose.   c. to form.

4 **decipher**
(dĭ-sī′fər)
-*verb*

- Why do contracts have to use language that's so difficult to **decipher**?
- On one of Holly's essays, her English teacher wrote, "Please type your papers. I can't **decipher** your handwriting."

a *Decipher* means   a. to figure out.   b. to find.   c. to improve.

5 **default**
(dĭ-fôlt′)
-*verb*

- We won our case against the appliance repairman because he **defaulted** by failing to appear in court.
- Jay's mother said, "I'll co-sign on your car loan, but you have to make every payment. If you **default**, it will hurt my credit rating."

b *Default* means   a. to act as expected.   b. not to do something required.   c. to begin.

6 **hypothetical**
(hī′pō-thĕt′ĭ-kəl)
-*adjective*

- Imagine the **hypothetical** situation of going to live alone on an island. Which books and music tapes would you take along?
- Law schools hold pretend court sessions with **hypothetical** cases so that students can practice their skills.

c *Hypothetical* means   a. sure to happen.   b. dangerous.   c. imaginary.

7 nominal
(nŏm′ə-nəl)
-adjective

- Except for a **nominal** registration fee, the camp for needy children is entirely free.
- Professor Banks gave us only **nominal** extra credit for participating in psychology experiments. She wanted our course grade to be based mainly on our test scores.

_b_ *Nominal* means   a. enormous.   b. very little.   c. helpful.

8 predominant
(prĭ-dŏm′ə-nənt)
-adjective

- Rock is the **predominant** music in our dorm, but country music is also popular.
- Although the **predominant** type of car in New York City in 1900 used gasoline, a third of the cars ran on electricity.

_b_ *Predominant* means   a. rare.   b. main.   c. temporary.

9 prerequisite
(pre-rĕk′wĭ-zĭt)
-noun

- You can't take Spanish Literature I unless you've taken the **prerequisite**, Spanish III.
- Being allergic to cigarette smoke, Kathy told Joel that his quitting smoking was a **prerequisite** for their marrying.

_a_ *Prerequisite* means   a. a requirement.   b. a penalty.   c. a method.

10 recession
(rĭ-sĕsh′ən)
-noun

- While seashore businesses in the North suffer a **recession** in the winter, they do very well from spring to fall.
- The department store laid off twenty workers during the **recession**, but it rehired them when business improved.

_c_ *Recession* means   a. a rapid growth.   b. a sale.   c. an economic setback.

Matching Words with Definitions

Following are definitions of the ten words. Clearly write or print each word next to its definition. The sentences above and on the previous page will help you decide on the meaning of each word.

1. _____constitute_____   a. To make up; be the parts of

2. _____default_____   b. To fail to do something required

3. _____predominant_____   c. Most common or most noticeable

4. _____prerequisite_____   d. Something required beforehand

5. _____confiscate_____   e. To seize with authority; legally take possession of

6. _____decipher_____   f. To interpret or read (something confusing or hard to make out)

7. _____nominal_____   g. Slight; very small compared with what might be expected

8. _____concurrent_____   h. Happening or existing at the same time; simultaneous

9. _____recession_____   i. A temporary decline in business

10. _____hypothetical_____   j. Supposed for the sake of argument or examination; imaginary; theoretical

CAUTION: Do not go any further until you are sure the above answers are correct. Then you can use the definitions to help you in the following practices. Your goal is eventually to know the words well enough so that you don't need to check the definitions at all.

➤ Sentence Check 1

Using the answer line provided, complete each item below with the correct word from the box. Use each word once.

a. concurrent	b. confiscate	c. constitute	d. decipher	e. default
f. hypothetical	g. nominal	h. predominant	i. prerequisite	j. recession

predominant 1. Anger was the ___ emotion among students when they first heard that their tuition would be raised again.

concurrent 2. Although the two robberies were ___—both occurred at midnight on Friday—one man had planned them both.

constitute 3. One hundred senators and 435 members of the House of Representatives ___ the United States Congress.

prerequisite 4. A ___ for taking the driver-education class is passing a written test on the driving laws.

nominal 5. The town library charges only a ___ fine for late books but a higher fine for late videotapes.

decipher 6. Karim has such terrible handwriting that his wife couldn't ___ his message saying she should meet him at the restaurant.

recession 7. When the shoe factory closed, our little town went into a ___ because the laid-off workers had no money to spend at local businesses.

default 8. The phone company refused to install a phone in Glen's new apartment because he had ___(e)d on several of his previous bills.

confiscate 9. One of the town's police officers ___s illegal fireworks from teenagers and then sets them off at his own home on the Fourth of July.

hypothetical 10. To teach young children safety, many parents explain what to do in ___ situations, such as if a stranger asks them to go for a ride.

NOTE: Now check your answers to these questions by turning to page 127. Going over the answers carefully will help you prepare for the next two practices, for which answers are not given.

➤ Sentence Check 2

Using the answer lines provided, complete each item below with **two** words from the box. Use each word once.

nominal
concurrent 1–2. This summer, local children can sign up for art or music lessons for a ___ fee of $3. It's impossible to take both, though, since the classes will be ___.

constitute
predominant 3–4. Although cancer and heart disease ___ the leading threats to life in the United States, car accidents are the ___ cause of death for teenagers.

_____ *prerequisite* _____   5–6. "It seems as if a degree in accounting is a ___ for understanding our tax laws," said Ken. "How else could anyone ___ the tax codes?"

_____ *decipher* _____

_____ *default* _____   7–8. The small print on my mortgage stated that if I should ___ on payments, the bank had the right to ___ my house.

_____ *confiscate* _____

_____ *hypothetical* _____   9–10. When Ms. Howe was interviewed for the job of store manager, the regional manager asked her a question about a ___ situation. "Imagine that our business is in a ___," he said. "What would you do to enhance° sales?"

_____ *recession* _____

➤ *Final Check:* Money Problems

Here is a final opportunity for you to strengthen your knowledge of the ten words. First read the following selection carefully. Then fill in each blank with a word from the box at the top of the previous page. (Context clues will help you figure out which word goes in which blank.) Use each word once.

"My car has been stolen!" My neighbor, Martha, ran into my house crying and angry. "I saw them take it."

I called the police for her, and she told an officer the license number and car model. "The (1)_____ *predominant* _____ color of the car is brown," she added, "but it has a black roof. I had it parked in the lot adjacent° to the beauty shop I own. I saw two men tow it away."

"You saw them tow it?" the officer asked. "Have you (2)_____ *default* _____(e)d on your car loan?"

"What do you mean?" Martha asked.

"If you haven't been making your payments, the bank or dealer has the right to (3)_____ *confiscate* _____ the car."

Martha admitted that she hadn't made any payments for three months. Later she told me she'd gotten notices in the mail but threw them away because their language was too complicated to (4)_____ *decipher* _____. She also said she was having money problems. (5)_____ *Concurrent* _____ with the car loan was a big home improvement loan. She also had five credit-card bills and regular living expenses to pay. To top it all off, the city was suffering from a (6)_____ *recession* _____, so her income was down, something her laid-off employees could certainly attest° to. She was about $12,000 in debt.

At my suggestion, Martha visited a debt counselor who helped her develop a comprehensive° plan to pay her bills. The only (7)_____ *prerequisite* _____s for this free service were a regular job and a willingness to pay one's debts in full. The counselor and Martha planned what would (8)_____ *constitute* _____ a reasonable budget, based on Martha's income and expenses. They then wrote to the companies she owed to arrange to pay a (9)_____ *nominal* _____ amount each month until the whole debt was paid. They also discussed what she would do in several (10)_____ *hypothetical* _____ situations, such as if her refrigerator died or her income changed.

Now, Martha is getting back on her feet again—in more ways than one, since she never got the car back.

Scores	Sentence Check 2 _____ %	Final Check _____ %

Enter your scores above and in the vocabulary performance chart on the inside back cover of the book.

degenerate	sanctuary
implausible	scrutiny
incoherent	sinister
intercede	suffice
intricate	vulnerable

Ten Words in Context

In the space provided, write the letter of the meaning closest to that of each **boldfaced** word. Use the context of the sentences to help you figure out each word's meaning.

1 degenerate
(dĭ-jĕn′ər-āt′)
-verb

• Mr. Freedman's family was called to the nursing home when the old man's condition began to **degenerate**. It was feared he didn't have long to live.

• Mel's relationship with his parents **degenerated** when he dropped out of school against their wishes and became a bartender.

_c_ *Degenerate* means   a. to improve.   b. to remain the same.   c. to worsen.

2 implausible
(ĭm-plô′zə-bəl)
-adjective

• As **implausible** as it may sound, Southern Florida sometimes does get snow.

• Insurance companies hear such **implausible** excuses for auto accidents as "I hit the telephone pole when I was blinded by the lights of a flying saucer."

_a_ *Implausible* means   a. unbelievable.   b. acceptable.   c. valuable.

3 incoherent
(ĭn′kō-hîr′ənt)
-adjective

• If Mitch drinks much more, he'll become completely **incoherent**. He's already having trouble expressing his thoughts clearly.

• My sister talks a lot in her sleep, but she's so **incoherent** then that we can never figure out what she's saying.

_b_ *Incoherent* means   a. calm.   b. unclear.   c. inconvenient.

4 intercede
(ĭn′tər-sēd′)
-verb

• When the principal said Harry couldn't play in Friday's football game, the coach **interceded**, hoping to change the principal's mind.

• Inez's parents refused to come to her wedding until her brother **interceded** and persuaded them to come after all.

_b_ *Intercede* means   a. to give in to someone.   b. to plead for someone.   c. to examine closely.

5 intricate
(ĭn′trĭ-kĭt)
-adjective

• *War and Peace* is a long, **intricate** novel that weaves together the detailed life stories of many individuals.

• It's amazing to see the **intricate** gold and silver jewelry that ancient Indians made with only simple tools. It obviously required great patience and skill to create such complex ornaments.

_c_ *Intricate* means   a. simple.   b. uninteresting.   c. complicated.

6 sanctuary
(săngk′chōō-ĕr′ē)
-noun

• Old, unused trains in Grand Central Station serve as a nighttime **sanctuary** for some of New York City's homeless.

• When the houseful of children becomes too noisy, Ned finds the laundry room to be a **sanctuary**, a place where he can read in quiet.

_b_ *Sanctuary* means   a. a reminder.   b. a shelter.   c. a challenge.

7 scrutiny
(skro͞ot′ən-ē)
-*noun*

- Store security guards give careful **scrutiny** to people carrying large bags, since the bags may be used for shoplifting.
- Before being published, a book comes under the **scrutiny** of a proofreader, who examines it for grammar and spelling errors.

_a_ *Scrutiny* means   a. attention.   b. protection.   c. permission.

8 sinister
(sĭn′ĭs-tər)
-*adjective*

- In the movie, a mad scientist thought up the **sinister** scheme of releasing a deadly virus. His evil plot failed when he died from the virus himself.
- Jack the Ripper, one of the more **sinister** criminals in English history, slashed the throats of six women.

_b_ *Sinister* means   a. illogical.   b. evil.   c. inconsiderate.

9 suffice
(sə-fīs′)
-*verb*

- The amount of research you've done may **suffice** for a high school term paper, but not for a college one.
- I forgot to buy something for lunch tomorrow, but the leftover meatloaf will **suffice**.

_b_ *Suffice* means   a. to be wasted.   b. to be adequate.   c. to be examined.

10 vulnerable
(vŭl′nər-ə-bəl)
-*adjective*

- Homes in heavily wooded areas are especially **vulnerable** to termites.
- Because they tend to have brittle bones, the elderly are **vulnerable** to fractures.

_a_ *Vulnerable* means   a. open.   b. safe.   c. attracted.

Matching Words with Definitions

Following are definitions of the ten words. Clearly write or print each word next to its definition. The sentences above and on the previous page will help you decide on the meaning of each word.

1. _____intricate_____   a. Having many parts arranged in a complicated way; complex

2. _____suffice_____   b. To be good enough

3. _____degenerate_____   c. To worsen; deteriorate

4. _____sanctuary_____   d. A place of safety, protection, or relief

5. _____intercede_____   e. To make a request or plead on behalf of someone else

6. _____vulnerable_____   f. Open to damage or attack; susceptible

7. _____implausible_____   g. Difficult to believe; unlikely

8. _____sinister_____   h. Evil; wicked

9. _____scrutiny_____   i. Close inspection; careful examination

10. _____incoherent_____   j. Unable to speak in an orderly, logical way

CAUTION: Do not go any further until you are sure the above answers are correct. Then you can use the definitions to help you in the following practices. Your goal is eventually to know the words well enough so that you don't need to check the definitions at all.

➤ *Sentence Check 1*

Using the answer line provided, complete each item below with the correct word from the box. Use each word once.

a. **degenerate**	b. **implausible**	c. **incoherent**	d. **intercede**	e. **intricate**
f. **sanctuary**	g. **scrutiny**	h. **sinister**	i. **suffice**	j. **vulnerable**

suffice   1. Ken's cartoons ___ for the school newspaper, but they wouldn't be good enough for the city papers.

sinister   2. The Joker's name is misleading, for he's a(n) ___ man who takes pleasure in doing evil.

vulnerable   3. People who live in big cities are more ___ to muggings than are residents of small towns.

intricate   4. The leaves outside the window created a(n) ___ lacy shadow on my bedroom wall.

implausible   5. Although it seems ___, the seemingly dead desert really does blossom after a rainstorm.

sanctuary   6. People who allow an escaped convict to use their home as a ___ may face criminal charges themselves.

incoherent   7. My husband was so upset that he was ___. It wasn't until he calmed down that I understood he had been fired.

scrutiny   8. Unclaimed bags at airports receive the ___ of security officers watching for drugs or explosives.

degenerate   9. When I don't have company, my apartment tends to ___ into a jumble of papers, clothes, and school supplies.

intercede   10. When Dad informed my little sister that she had to be home from her date no later than ten o'clock, Mom ___(e)d and got her a midnight curfew.

NOTE: Now check your answers to these questions by turning to page 127. Going over the answers carefully will help you prepare for the next two practices, for which answers are not given.

➤ *Sentence Check 2*

Using the answer lines provided, complete each item below with **two** words from the box. Use each word once.

vulnerable
sanctuary   1–2. Birds feel ___ to attack when they are out in the open. To attract them to your bird feeder, put it near a ___ of thickly growing trees and large bushes.

implausible
suffice   3–4. To get into the party, Mitch made up a flagrant° lie—a(n) ___ story about having lost our invitations in a fire. Surprisingly, the unlikely tale ___(e)d to get us in.

_____ *intricate* _____   5–6. When a complicated musical piece is played by a talented orchestra,
_____ *degenerate* _____   audiences can appreciate the ___ structure. But when poor musicians try
the piece, it ___s into nothing more than noise.

_____ *sinister* _____   7–8. As he left the bank, the robber shot an elderly man on mere impulse.
_____ *incoherent* _____   Shocked by the ___ act, the bank clerk was at first ___. However, after
calming down, she was able to clearly tell the police about the robbery
and the totally arbitrary° shooting.

_____ *scrutiny* _____   9–10. The children's eager ___ of the carefully arranged candies and cookies
_____ *intercede* _____   brought a warning from their mother: "Look, but don't touch!"
However, their grandmother ___(e)d and convinced her that it would be
unfair to give all the goodies to company and none to the children.

➤ *Final Check:* **The New French Employee**

Here is a final opportunity for you to strengthen your knowledge of the ten words. First read the following selection carefully. Then fill in each blank with a word from the box at the top of the previous page. (Context clues will help you figure out which word goes in which blank.) Use each word once.

One summer, Nan worked in a factory with an employee who had recently arrived from France, a soft-spoken young man named Jean-Louis. He spoke little English, but Nan's basic French (1)_____ *suffice* _____(e)d for simple conversations and helpful translations.

However, one day when she was called to the foreman's office, she wished she knew no French at all. FBI agents were there with Jean-Louis. After explaining that Jean-Louis may have been more (2)_____ *sinister* _____ than the innocent young man he appeared to be, the foreman left her there to translate for the agents. The agents said Jean-Louis had been on the run after committing several jewel thefts in France. Nan struggled to translate their questions, which were often too (3)_____ *intricate* _____ for her limited vocabulary. At times, she became so nervous that she was nearly (4)_____ *incoherent* _____. When Jean-Louis finally deciphered° what Nan was saying, he said the police were maligning° him. He claimed he was being mistaken for his no-good twin brother, who was responsible for the robberies. The angry FBI agents found Jean-Louis's story (5)_____ *implausible* _____. The conversation soon (6)_____ *degenerate* _____(e)d into a shouting match, with everyone yelling at poor Nan. When her boss heard the racket, he (7)_____ *intercede* _____(e)d, appeased° the agents, and got them to excuse her.

Nan then went to the ladies' room, a (8)_____ *sanctuary* _____ from the turmoil° of all the shouting. After the agents left with Jean-Louis, she was calm enough to go back to work. But she felt (9)_____ *vulnerable* _____ for days as she wondered if she was under the (10)_____ *scrutiny* _____ of jewel thieves who might blame her for Jean-Louis's arrest.

Scores Sentence Check 2 _____% Final Check _____%

Enter your scores above and in the vocabulary performance chart on the inside back cover of the book.

CHAPTER 8

blatant	gloat
blight	immaculate
contrive	plagiarism
garble	qualm
gaunt	retaliate

Ten Words in Context

In the space provided, write the letter of the meaning closest to that of each **boldfaced** word. Use the context of the sentences to help you figure out each word's meaning.

1 blatant
(blā′tənt)
-adjective

- Scott's smoking is **blatant**. Not only does he light up everywhere, but his clothes smell of smoke, and his fingers are stained with nicotine.
- The company's disregard of the environment is **blatant**. It makes no effort to stop polluting coastal waters with garbage.

a *Blatant* means   a. unmistakable.   b. scrambled.   c. not noticeable.

2 blight
(blīt)
-noun

- Nothing has hurt our country more than the **blight** of drugs.
- There are two ways of looking at TV: as a **blight** that dulls the mind or as a valuable source of information.

c *Blight* means   a. something that assists.   b. something very obvious.   c. something that harms.

3 contrive
(kən′trīv)
-verb

- My eight-year-old son could write a book titled *101 Ways I Have **Contrived** to Stay Up Past My Bedtime*.
- Jill has to **contrive** a way to get a day off from work for her friend's wedding. She's already used up her vacation time.

a *Contrive* means   a. to think up.   b. to mix up.   c. to avoid.

4 garble
(gär′bəl)
-verb

- The typesetter accidentally **garbled** the newspaper story, giving the reader only a mixed-up article.
- The company had **garbled** the bike's assembly instructions so badly that we were constantly confused about which step to do next.

c *Garble* means   a. to read.   b. to lose.   c. to jumble.

5 gaunt
(gônt)
-adjective

- Abraham Lincoln's beard made his **gaunt** face look fuller.
- Sharon's eating disorder, called anorexia nervosa, has made her so **gaunt** that she looks like a walking skeleton.

a *Gaunt* means   a. very thin.   b. wide.   c. confused.

6 gloat
(glōt)
-verb

- The coach told his team, "There's only one thing worse than a sore loser, and that's a mean winner. Don't **gloat**."
- Neil's sister always tattles on him and then **gloats** when he's punished, saying, "I told you so."

b *Gloat* means   a. to apologize fully.   b. to be overly self-satisfied.   c. to pay back.

7 immaculate
(ĭ-măk′yə-lĭt)
-*adjective*

- It's amazing that while Carolyn always appears **immaculate**, her apartment often seems very dirty.
- Don't expect a child to come home from a birthday party with **immaculate** clothing. Children usually manage to get as much birthday cake on their clothing as in their mouths.

_b_ *Immaculate* means   a. uncomfortable.   b. spotless.   c. soiled.

8 plagiarism
(plā′jĕ-rĭz′əm)
-*noun*

- When the author saw a movie with the same plot as one of her novels, she sued for **plagiarism**.
- The teacher warned her students that using an author's exact words as one's own is **plagiarism**.

_b_ *Plagiarism* means   a. creativity.   b. the stealing of ideas.   c. planning.

9 qualm
(kwŏm)
-*noun*

- Larry had no **qualms** about stealing from the cafeteria cash register. He didn't even feel guilty when someone else was blamed.
- After hiding Lori's bike as an April Fool's joke, I began to have **qualms**. What if she thought it was stolen and called the police?

_a_ *Qualm* means   a. a guilty feeling.   b. a proud memory.   c. a clever plan.

10 retaliate
(rĭ-tăl′ē-āt′)
-*verb*

- When I broke my sister's stereo, she **retaliated** by cutting the cord of my Sony Walkman earphones.
- When Mary told about Flo's secret love affair, Flo **retaliated** by telling their friends about Mary's shoplifting.

_b_ *Retaliate* means   a. to forgive.   b. to take revenge.   c. to confuse.

Matching Words with Definitions

Following are definitions of the ten words. Clearly write or print each word next to its definition. The sentences above and on the previous page will help you decide on the meaning of each word.

1. _____qualm_____   a. An uneasy feeling about how right or proper a particular action is
2. _____garble_____   b. To mix up or confuse (as a story or message); scramble
3. _____gloat_____   c. To feel or express delight or self-satisfaction, often spitefully
4. _____blight_____   d. Something that weakens, damages, or destroys
5. _____plagiarism_____   e. Using someone else's writings or ideas as one's own
6. _____contrive_____   f. To plan cleverly; think up
7. _____retaliate_____   g. To return an injury for an injury; pay back
8. _____blatant_____   h. Very obvious, often offensively so
9. _____immaculate_____   i. Perfectly clean
10. _____gaunt_____   j. Thin and bony

CAUTION: Do not go any further until you are sure the above answers are correct. Then you can use the definitions to help you in the following practices. Your goal is eventually to know the words well enough so that you don't need to check the definitions at all.

➤ Sentence Check 1

Using the answer line provided, complete each item below with the correct word from the box. Use each word once.

a. **blatant**	b. **blight**	c. **contrive**	d. **garble**	e. **gaunt**
f. **gloat**	g. **immaculate**	h. **plagiarism**	i. **qualm**	j. **retaliate**

immaculate   1. A(n) ___ house may be a sign that someone has nothing better to do than clean.

blight   2. Child abuse is an awful ___ on the physical and mental health of our youth.

gloat   3. My aunt refuses to drive Mr. Elson to bingo because he ___s so much when he wins, which is often.

blatant   4. The F's and D's on my brother's report card are ___ evidence of how little he has studied this term.

contrive   5. Emilio still hopes to ___ a way to get Rita to go out with him, even though she's refused him four times.

garble   6. I bought an answering machine because my children have ___(e)d several important phone messages.

retaliate   7. Every time the Hatfields harmed the McCoys, the McCoys would ___, so the feud went on for years.

gaunt   8. Rescued after being lost at sea for nine days, the men were terribly ___, but they put on weight rapidly.

qualm   9. I would feel guilty if I called in sick when I wasn't, but no one else in the office seems to have any ___s about doing that.

plagiarism   10. Mark Twain joked that charges of ___ were ridiculous because no one can be completely original. He wrote, "We mortals can't create—we can only copy."

NOTE: Now check your answers to these questions by turning to page 127. Going over the answers carefully will help you prepare for the next two practices, for which answers are not given.

➤ Sentence Check 2

Using the answer lines provided, complete each item below with **two** words from the box. Use each word once.

immaculate
blatant   1–2. The living room looked ___ except for a lump under the carpet, a(n) ___ sign that my son had taken a shortcut in cleaning up.

retaliate
qualm   3–4. After the bully struck him, Jules wanted to ___ by throwing a rock, but he had ___s about doing anything so dangerous.

_____gaunt_____ 5–6. My little girl was so ___ after her illness that I carefully ___(e)d fattening meals that were sure to arouse her appetite.

_____contrive_____

_____plagiarism_____ 7–8. "At least I know you aren't guilty of ___," said my teacher. "Nobody else would have ___(e)d the report so badly that it's impossible to follow."

_____garble_____

_____blight_____ 9–10. Willie is a ___ on our school. Not only does he start fights with opposing players on the basketball court, but he also ___s after he's benched, as if he's proud of causing such turmoil°. In fact, although he's a great player, the coach is pondering° kicking him off the team.

_____gloat_____

➤ _Final Check:_ A Cruel Teacher

Here is a final opportunity for you to strengthen your knowledge of the ten words. First read the following selection carefully. Then fill in each blank with a word from the box at the top of the previous page. (Context clues will help you figure out which word goes in which blank.) Use each word once.

It has been twenty years since I was in Mr. Brill's tenth-grade biology class, but I still get nervous thinking about it. Mr. Brill was a tall, (1)_____gaunt_____ man who resembled the skeleton at the back of the room. His meanness was (2)_____blatant_____. For his most difficult questions, he would call on the shyest kids, those most vulnerable° to the pain of embarrassment. And when they nervously (3)_____garble_____(e)d their answers, he would (4)_____gloat_____, as if their poor performance were a personal victory for him. The discomfort of some of his victims was almost tangible°, nearly as solid as the wooden pointer he sometimes slammed across his desk just to shock us. He seemed to (5)_____contrive_____ situations just to make us miserable. For example, if our fingernails were not (6)_____immaculate_____, we were sent out of class. As if we needed clean hands to dissect a frog! One time I worked extremely hard on a paper for class, but he accused me of (7)_____plagiarism_____. He said I must have copied it because I was too dumb to write anything that good. Without a (8)_____qualm_____, he gave me an F, which ruined my average and discouraged me for the rest of the year. All of us students would imagine ways to get even with him, but we were too afraid to (9)_____retaliate_____. Why a teacher like that was allowed to continue teaching was an enigma° to us, one I still have not figured out. In all the years since, I've never met a person who was such a (10)_____blight_____ on the teaching profession.

Scores	Sentence Check 2 _____%	Final Check _____%

Enter your scores above and in the vocabulary performance chart on the inside back cover of the book.

CHAPTER

9

curtail	indispensable
devastate	intermittent
digress	rigor
incentive	squander
incorporate	succumb

Ten Words in Context

In the space provided, write the letter of the meaning closest to that of each **boldfaced** word. Use the context of the sentences to help you figure out each word's meaning.

1 curtail
(kər-tāl′)
-verb

- Upon hearing reports of a tornado, our boss **curtailed** the meeting so we all could go home early.
- I need to **curtail** my volunteer activities so that I can spend more time earning money to pay back a loan.

_b_ *Curtail* means
a. to combine.   b. to shorten.   c. to extend.

2 devastate
(dĕv′əs-tāt′)
-verb

- Learning that their son had been arrested for armed robbery **devastated** the Huttons. They couldn't believe he'd do such a terrible thing.
- Vera is so fond of Andy. She'll be **devastated** to hear he has cancer.

_c_ *Devastate* means
a. to thrill.   b. to annoy.   c. to upset greatly.

3 digress
(dī-grĕs′)
-verb

- Professor Rubin never **digresses** during a lecture. Even his jokes relate to the day's topic.
- I tried teaching my three-year-old his phone number, but we **digressed** to a discussion of whether Winnie the Pooh has a telephone.

_b_ *Digress* means
a. to listen carefully.   b. to go off the subject.   c. to get up.

4 incentive
(ĭn′sĕn′tĭv)
-noun

- The insurance company offers an **incentive**—a free vacation—to encourage its representatives to make more sales.
- The thought of myself in a bathing suit next summer provides me with an adequate **incentive** to exercise.

_a_ *Incentive* means
a. encouragement.   b. liberty.   c. change.

5 incorporate
(ĭn-kôr′pər-āt′)
-verb

- Jerry **incorporated** all of his favorite desserts into one: a chocolate-covered banana-cream pecan pie.
- Since the number of young children has gone down in my neighborhood, the two elementary schools have been **incorporated** into one.

_b_ *Incorporate* means
a. to give up.   b. to join together.   c. to raise.

6 indispensable
(ĭn-dĭ-spĕn′sə-bəl)
-adjective

- Because there's no bus or train service nearby, a car is **indispensable** in my neighborhood.
- When you're broke, you find that many things you thought were **indispensable** aren't actually necessary after all.

_b_ *Indispensable* means
a. free.   b. needed.   c. expensive.

7 **intermittent**
(ĭn′tər-mĭt′ənt)
-*adjective*

- You have to work steadily with your dog to train him well. **Intermittent** practice won't work.
- Dora realized that weight loss would be **intermittent** when she dieted, so she didn't give up when the losses stopped and started.

<u>a</u> *Intermittent* means   a. irregular.   b. too much.   c. steady.

8 **rigor**
(rĭg′ər)
-*noun*

- New Marines must go through the **rigors** of boot camp, such as completing an obstacle course and running several miles a day.
- The **rigor** of working at two part-time jobs while going to school proved too much for Joseph. Exhausted, he dropped both jobs.

<u>c</u> *Rigor* means   a. a gamble.   b. an expense.   c. a hardship.

9 **squander**
(skwŏn′dər)
-*verb*

- It's sad to see such a wonderful artist **squander** her talent designing labels for baked-bean cans.
- The company lunchroom now closes promptly at one o'clock so that workers can't **squander** time on long lunch breaks.

<u>b</u> *Squander* means   a. to share.   b. to misuse.   c. to upset.

10 **succumb**
(sə-kŭm′)
-*verb*

- Leah **succumbed** to her daughter's begging and bought her a pet lizard for her birthday.
- Once the suspect was arrested, he quickly **succumbed** and confessed to stealing the car stereo.

<u>a</u> *Succumb* means   a. to yield.   b. to delay.   c. to anger.

Matching Words with Definitions

Following are definitions of the ten words. Clearly write or print each word next to its definition. The sentences above and on the previous page will help you decide on the meaning of each word.

1. _squander_ a. To waste; spend or use foolishly
2. _curtail_ b. To cut short or reduce
3. _incentive_ c. Something that moves one to take action or work harder; a motivation
4. _digress_ d. To turn aside, or stray, especially from the main topic in speaking or writing
5. _rigor_ e. Great hardship or difficulty; harshness; severity
6. _devastate_ f. To upset deeply; overwhelm
7. _succumb_ g. To give in; stop resisting
8. _indispensable_ h. Necessary
9. _incorporate_ i. To unite into a single whole; combine
10. _intermittent_ j. Starting and stopping from time to time; off-and-on

CAUTION: Do not go any further until you are sure the above answers are correct. Then you can use the definitions to help you in the following practices. Your goal is eventually to know the words well enough so that you don't need to check the definitions at all.

➤ *Sentence Check 1*

Using the answer line provided, complete each item below with the correct word from the box. Use each word once.

a. **curtail**	b. **devastate**	c. **digress**	d. **incentive**	e. **incorporate**
f. **indispensable**	g. **intermittent**	h. **rigor**	i. **squander**	j. **succumb**

Intermittent　　1. ___ rain kept interrupting the ballgame.

devastate　　2. The sight of her bandaged husband in an oxygen tent ___(e)d Claire.

incorporate　　3. Someone has managed to ___ a tomato and a potato into one plant.

indispensable　　4. A home computer and a telephone are ___ tools for many self-employed people.

incentive　　5. Airlines offer "frequent flyer credits" toward free trips as an ___ to get people to fly often.

rigor　　6. Many teenagers don't foresee the ___s of parenthood, such as staying up all night with a sick child.

squander　　7. By examining her last two months of spending, Coretta discovered that she had ___(e)d money on too many expensive meals.

curtail　　8. The man on the corner offered to sell me a watch, but he quickly ___(e)d his sales pitch when he saw a police officer approaching.

digress　　9. Because our history teacher loved to gab, we often could get him to ___ from the lesson to talk about school athletics or school politics.

succumb　　10. Carl resisted Lola's charms for months, thinking she was too young for him, but he finally ___(e)d and asked her out to dinner.

NOTE: Now check your answers to these questions by turning to page 128. Going over the answers carefully will help you prepare for the next two practices, for which answers are not given.

➤ *Sentence Check 2*

Using the answer lines provided, complete each item below with **two** words from the box. Use each word once.

squander
rigor　　1–2. Duane feels he ___(e)d too many years in inactivity, so now he welcomes the ___s of an exercise program.

curtail
incorporate　　3–4. The company decided to ___ the construction of its new plant until the architects could decide on how to ___ an employee gym into the new building.

intermittent
succumb　　5–6. My aunt has only ___ success in quitting smoking. Every few months she___s to temptation, and then she has to quit all over again.

_____devastate_____   7–8. As Leo explained a failed business deal that had once ___(e)d him, he
_____digress_____   ___(e)d into the even more interesting tale of his romance with Molly,
                                  his business partner.

_____incentive_____   9–10. The vitamin saleswoman offered me free samples, ninety-day trials, and
_____indispensable_____   every other ___ she could think of to get me to buy. However, I found
                                  her sales pitch highly implausible°. I simply could not believe that her
                                  products, and her products alone, were ___ to my well-being.

➤ Final Check: Learning to Study

Here is a final opportunity for you to strengthen your knowledge of the ten words. First read the following selection carefully. Then fill in each blank with a word from the box at the top of the previous page. (Context clues will help you figure out which word goes in which blank.) Use each word once.

Linda never had to work very hard to make good grades in high school. But in college, where the (1)_____rigor_____s of course work were greater, her casual high-school study habits would no longer suffice°. It was also much easier in college for Linda to (2)_____squander_____ time on dates and parties. She didn't realize how badly she was doing until she saw her midterm grades, which (3)_____devastate_____(e)d her. She knew she had to make some changes right away and began to ponder° what they should be. As a(n) (4)_____incentive_____ to work harder, she tried studying with her friend Denise. But that didn't work; their conversation would (5)_____digress_____ from European history to personal topics, such as dates or favorite singers.

Linda decided she'd have to go it alone. She began to skip weekday parties and also to (6)_____curtail_____ the time she spent talking with friends. She discovered that a good place to study was (7)_____indispensable_____ to her new study habits. She found the library's silent third floor a sanctuary°, a place with no temptations to which she could (8)_____succumb_____. She also became more methodical° in her study habits, keeping an assignment book, writing due dates on a calendar, and setting up a study schedule. At first, Linda's performance fluctuated°, and so the improvement in her grades was (9)_____intermittent_____—A's and B's alternated with C's and D's. But little by little, she learned to (10)_____incorporate_____ a social life with serious study and get grades she was proud of.

Scores	Sentence Check 2 _____%	Final Check _____%

Enter your scores above and in the vocabulary performance chart on the inside back cover of the book.

alleviate	infamous
benefactor	intrinsic
covert	revulsion
cynic	speculate
demise	virile

Ten Words in Context

In the space provided, write the letter of the meaning closest to that of each **boldfaced** word. Use the context of the sentences to help you figure out each word's meaning.

1 alleviate
(ə-lē′vē-āt′)
-verb

- To **alleviate** his loneliness, the widower moved closer to his daughter and her family.
- After a long game in the August heat, the young baseball players **alleviated** their thirst with ice-cold lemonade.

_c_ *Alleviate* means   a. to consider.   b. to hide.   c. to ease.

2 benefactor
(běn′ə-făk′tər)
-noun

- The Second Street Bank is a long-time **benefactor** of the arts. This year it will sponsor a series of free jazz concerts in the parks.
- The wealthy **benefactor** who paid for the child's operation prefers to remain anonymous.

_a_ *Benefactor* means   a. a financial supporter.   b. a social critic.   c. a cooperative person.

3 covert
(kŭv′ərt)
-adjective

- Miriam and David's relationship is so **covert** that they never eat out. Even Miriam's parents don't know she is seeing him.
- If you enjoy **covert** activities, become a secret agent.

_b_ *Covert* means   a. obvious.   b. concealed.   c. easy to bear.

4 cynic
(sĭn′ĭk)
-noun

- Her parents' nasty divorce has made Libby a **cynic** about marriage.
- Mr. Bryant was a **cynic** about people until he fell down on a street corner and several strangers rushed to his aid.

_a_ *Cynic* means   a. someone who believes the worst.   b. someone who gives help.   c. someone with a bad reputation.

5 demise
(dĭ-mīz′)
-noun

- Drugs have led to the **demise** of numerous athletes, such as the great basketball player Len Bias.
- In 1567, a beard caused a man's **demise**. Hans Steininger's beard was so long that he stepped on it while climbing a staircase, lost his balance, fell down the steps, and died.

_c_ *Demise* means   a. popularity.   b. secret.   c. dying.

6 infamous
(ĭn′fə-məs)
-adjective

- King Henry VIII of England was **infamous** throughout Europe for executing two of his six wives.
- Visitors to the dungeons of ancient castles always want to see the instruments of torture, including the **infamous** Iron Maiden—a body-shaped box with spikes inside.

_a_ *Infamous* means   a. known unfavorably.   b. thought to be annoying.   c. giving hope.

7 **intrinsic**
(ĭn-trĭn′sĭk)
-*adjective*

- Trust is **intrinsic** to any good friendship.
- Because Lian has an **intrinsic** desire to learn, she doesn't need the reward of good grades to motivate her studies.

_b_ *Intrinsic* means

    a. secret.   b. fundamental.   c. unnecessary.

8 **revulsion**
(rĭ-vŭl′shən)
-*noun*

- Whenever I read about child abuse in the newspaper, I am filled with such **revulsion** that I often cannot finish the article.
- When Sharon met the man who had cheated her father, she was overcome with **revulsion**.

_b_ *Revulsion* means

    a. interest.   b. hatred.   c. understanding.

9 **speculate**
(spĕk′yə-lāt′)
-*verb*

- It's interesting to **speculate** how history might have been different if Abraham Lincoln had lived a few years longer.
- The therapist asked Cassy to **speculate** about what might happen if she told Ralph her true feelings.

_c_ *Speculate* means

    a. to remember.   b. to announce.   c. to guess.

10 **virile**
(vîr′əl)
-*adjective*

- Men who are unsure about their masculinity sometimes try to "prove" they are **virile** by being overly aggressive.
- When a male heron stamps his feet and sticks his neck out, and then drops his head and says "plop-buzz," the female finds him very **virile**. In fact, that behavior is how the male attracts a mate.

_a_ *Virile* means

    a. having attractive male qualities.   b. lacking in confidence.   c. unselfish.

Matching Words with Definitions

Following are definitions of the ten words. Clearly write or print each word next to its definition. The sentences above and on the previous page will help you decide on the meaning of each word.

1. _____covert_____   a. Secret; hidden

2. _____cynic_____   b. A person who believes the worst of people's behavior and motives; someone who believes people are motivated only by selfishness

3. _____intrinsic_____   c. Belonging to a person or thing by its very nature (and thus not dependent on circumstances)

4. _____infamous_____   d. Having a very bad reputation; widely known for being vicious, criminal, or deserving of contempt

5. _____benefactor_____   e. A person or organization that gives help, especially financial aid

6. _____virile_____   f. Manly; masculine

7. _____demise_____   g. Death

8. _____speculate_____   h. To come up with ideas or theories about a subject; theorize

9. _____alleviate_____   i. To relieve; make easier to endure

10. _____revulsion_____   j. Great disgust or distaste

CAUTION: Do not go any further until you are sure the above answers are correct. Then you can use the definitions to help you in the following practices. Your goal is eventually to know the words well enough so that you don't need to check the definitions at all.

➤ *Sentence Check 1*

Using the answer line provided, complete each item below with the correct word from the box. Use each word once.

a. **alleviate**	b. **benefactor**	c. **covert**	d. **cynic**	e. **demise**
f. **infamous**	g. **intrinsic**	h. **revulsion**	i. **speculate**	j. **virile**

intrinsic   1. Problems are ___ to life; they're unavoidable.

alleviate   2. My hunger isn't fully satisfied, but the apple ___(e)d it somewhat.

virile   3. Teenage guys usually welcome a deepening voice and a thickening beard as signs that they are becoming more___.

cynic   4. The selfless work of the nuns in the slums of India is enough to touch the hearts of most hardened ___s.

infamous   5. Though she was tried and found not guilty, Lizzie Borden is still ___ for killing her parents with a hatchet.

covert   6. The children loved the ___ activities involved in preparing their mother's surprise party.

revulsion   7. The mass murderer's neighbors were overcome with ___ when they learned what their "friend" had been doing in his basement.

speculate   8. "As no group has claimed responsibility, we can only ___ on the motives for the bombing," said the newscaster.

benefactor   9. Roger Novak had been a well-known ___ of AIDS research, so it was no surprise that he left a lot of money for the research in his will.

demise   10. It's a good idea for married couples to discuss their funeral plans in case of each other's ___. For example, do they wish to be buried or cremated?

NOTE: Now check your answers to these questions by turning to page 128. Going over the answers carefully will help you prepare for the next two practices, for which answers are not given.

➤ *Sentence Check 2*

Using the answer lines provided, complete each item below with **two** words from the box. Use each word once.

intrinsic
alleviate   1–2. Nursing is a good career for Dee because it's a(n) ___ part of her personality to try to ___ people's pain. In addition, since she is physically and mentally strong, she will be able to handle the rigors° of nursing, such as intense stress and long hours.

revulsion
covert   3–4. Although everything about the Nazis filled the Dutch spy with ___, his ___ assignment was to make friends with top Nazi scientists. He had few qualms° about faking such friendships—he would have felt more guilty if he hadn't done everything in his power to fight the Nazis.

_____ cynic _____   5–6. The ___s in town said that Joyce Lester's sorrow over her husband's
_____ demise _____   ___ was much less than her joy in getting the money from his insurance
                          policy.

_____ virile _____   7–8. Young men who are bullies usually think of themselves ___, but a ___
_____ benefactor _____   of the weak is far more manly than someone who takes advantage of
                          weakness.

_____ infamous _____ 9–10. With all the stories told about Jesse James, the Dalton Gang, and other
_____ speculate _____   ___ figures of the Wild West, we can only ___ as to how much is fact
                          and how much is fiction.

➤ *Final Check:* **The Mad Monk**

Here is a final opportunity for you to strengthen your knowledge of the ten words. First read the following selection carefully. Then fill in each blank with a word from the box at the top of the previous page. (Context clues will help you figure out which word goes in which blank.) Use each word once.

Shortly before the Russian Revolution, an eccentric° man named Rasputin became (1)_____ infamous _____ as the "mad monk." Because he dressed like a peasant, drank heavily, and rarely bathed, the nobility often felt (2)_____ revulsion _____ when they encountered° him at the palace.

Yet despite his outward appearance, Rasputin possessed a(n) (3)_____ intrinsic _____ charm that drew many to him, including the Russian empress. She thought him a great man of God and a special (4)_____ benefactor _____ of her seriously ill son, whose condition she felt Rasputin (5)_____ alleviate _____(e)d.

Many (6)_____ cynic _____s believed otherwise. To them, Rasputin was no healer but a man who exploited° his relationship with the empress for his own benefit. Rather than praise Rasputin, his enemies preferred to malign° him. In a pamphlet titled *The Holy Devil*, one of his critics described him as a sinister° man. This author even dared to (7)_____ speculate _____ that the monk and the empress were romantically involved. This theory was strengthened by the fact that the empress's "holy man" pursued many women and boasted about how (8)_____ virile _____ he was.

Finally, a group of Russian noblemen made (9)_____ covert _____ plans to kill Rasputin. Somehow, the secret must have gotten out, for a Russian official warned Rasputin of a plot against him. He nevertheless accepted the noblemen's invitation to a dinner party, where they served him poisoned wine and cake. When Rasputin did not appear to succumb° to the poison, his enemies hastened his (10)_____ demise _____ by shooting and stabbing him and then dumping him into an icy river. An autopsy revealed that he had died by drowning.

| *Scores* | Sentence Check 2 ____% | Final Check ____% |

Enter your scores above and in the vocabulary performance chart on the inside back cover of the book.

UNIT TWO: Review

The box at the right lists twenty-five words from Unit Two. Using the clues at the bottom of the page, fill in these words to complete the puzzle that follows.

Word list:
- alleviate
- blight
- concurrent
- constitute
- covert
- curtail
- cynic
- decipher
- degenerate
- digress
- garble
- gaunt
- gloat
- intricate
- intrinsic
- nominal
- prerequisite
- qualm
- rigor
- scrutiny
- sinister
- squander
- succumb
- suffice
- virile

Completed puzzle answers:
- 2 CYNIC
- 3 COVERT (down)
- 4 INTRINSIC
- 1 BLIGHT (down)
- 6 QUALM (down)
- 7 SQUANDER
- 9 GLOAT
- 12 RIGOR
- 14 PREREQUISITE
- 16 SUFFICE
- 17 GARBLE
- 19 CONSTITUTE
- 20 DIGRESS
- 22 SUCCUMB
- 23 CURTAIL
- 24 SCRUTINY
- 5 VIRILE (down)
- 13 INTRICATE (down)
- 15 SINISTER (down)
- 18 DECIPHER (down)
- 21 GAUNT (down)
- 8 DEGENERATE (down)
- 10 ALLEVIATE (down)
- 11 NOMINAL (down)

ACROSS

2. A person who believes the worst of people's behavior and motives
4. Belonging to a person or thing by its very nature (and thus not dependent on circumstances)
7. To waste; spend or use foolishly
9. To feel or express delight or self-satisfaction, often spitefully
12. Great hardship or difficulty; harshness; severity
14. Something required beforehand
16. To be good enough
17. To mix up or confuse (as a story or message); scramble
19. To make up; be the parts of
20. To turn aside, or stray, especially from the main topic in speaking or writing
22. To give in; stop resisting
23. To cut short or reduce
24. Close inspection; careful examination

DOWN

1. Something that weakens, damages, or destroys
2. Happening or existing at the same time; simultaneous
3. Secret; hidden
5. Manly; masculine
6. An uneasy feeling about how right or proper a particular action is
8. To worsen; deteriorate
10. To relieve; make easier to endure
11. Slight; very small compared with what might be expected
13. Having parts arranged in a complicated way; complex
15. Evil; wicked
18. To interpret or read (something confusing or hard to make out)
21. Thin and bony

UNIT TWO: Test 1

PART A
Choose the word that best completes each item and write it in the space provided.

speculate   1. Scientists ___ that the average life span of a dinosaur was probably 100 to 120 years.
       a. speculate   b. digress   c. curtail   d. confiscate

degenerate   2. Unless figure skaters practice regularly, their skills will ___.
       a. retaliate   b. degenerate   c. confiscate   d. decipher

implausible   3. It may sound ___, but a camel can drink twenty-five gallons of water at a time.
       a. implausible   b. blatant   c. covert   d. virile

concurrent   4. Movie subtitles should be ___ with the spoken words they are translating.
       a. immaculate   b. infamous   c. incoherent   d. concurrent

immaculate   5. Even the most ___ people have microscopic creatures clinging to their hair.
       a. sinister   b. immaculate   c. incoherent   d. intricate

blight   6 Measles remains a serious ___ worldwide, killing over a million people each year.
       a. blight   b. plagiarism   c. qualm   d. prerequisite

curtailed   7. A power failure ___ our viewing of the TV mystery, so we never found out who had committed the murder.
       a. deciphered   b. curtailed   c. retaliated   d. speculated

default   8. The government student loan program is in serious trouble because many students ___ on their payments.
       a. suffice   b. alleviate   c. constitute   d. default

covert   9. The CIA's ___ activities often include "bugging" people's telephone lines with tiny, hidden microphones.
       a. blatant   b. virile   c. covert   d. immaculate

nominal   10. Although our college library charges only a(n) ___ fee to use a computer, I don't think it should charge students any fee at all.
       a. vulnerable   b. nominal   c. incoherent   d. sinister

(Continues on next page)

_____cynic_____ 11. Freud, being a(n) ___, believed that all people are driven primarily by selfish desires.

   a. prerequisite   b. blight   c. incentive   d. cynic

_____demise_____ 12. The ___ of a Connecticut man was strange indeed. He died when his five-hundred-pound wife sat on him.

   a. sanctuary   b. blight   c. benefactor   d. demise

PART B
Write **C** if the italicized word is used **correctly**. Write **I** if the word is used **incorrectly**.

__I__ 13. Our English teacher said, "Be sure to *digress*. A short essay needs a tight focus."

__C__ 14. Ocean plants *constitute* about 85 percent of all the greenery on Earth.

__I__ 15. Jesse Jackson is often praised for his *garbled* speeches.

__I__ 16. The beautiful sunset, with dramatic red swirls in a pink sky, filled us with *revulsion*.

__C__ 17. Elise enjoys *intricate* jigsaw puzzles, such as those of detailed flower displays.

__I__ 18. Vince *gloated* when he learned that his girlfriend was moving to another state.

__C__ 19. Knowing basic math skills is a *prerequisite* for learning the more advanced concepts of algebra.

__I__ 20. Adult dolphins often form a protective ring around young ones to keep them *vulnerable* from attack.

__C__ 21. Felix's teacher suspected him of *plagiarism* because his last paper was so much better written than his others.

__C__ 22. In a *blatant* case of injustice, a wealthy and influential North Carolina man received no punishment when he was caught selling cocaine.

__I__ 23. Fran often *squanders* her money by walking through rain or snow instead of paying for a cab.

__I__ 24. Each year, thousands of Americans who think themselves too *gaunt* have some fat surgically removed.

__C__ 25. Shortly before his birthday, Bruce *contrived* to get his parents to walk past the toy store so that he could point out the Nintendo game displayed in the window.

```
  Score   (Number correct) _____ x 4 = _____%
```

Enter your score above and in the vocabulary performance chart on the inside back cover of the book.

UNIT TWO: Test 2

PART A
Complete each item with a word from the box. Use each word once.

a. **alleviate**	b. **benefactor**	c. **confiscate**	d. **decipher**
e. **intermittent**	f. **qualm**	g. **retaliate**	h. **rigor**
i. **scrutiny**	j. **sinister**	k. **succumb**	l. **suffice**

intermittent   1. In irregular bursts of energy, dying stars give off ___ radio signals.

alleviate   2. The muscle ointment will ___ the pain of your sprained neck.

succumb   3. The owner of the restaurant ___(e)d to public pressure and established a nonsmoking section.

suffice   4. A hint to my daughter to take out the garbage won't ___. She needs to be told to do it.

decipher   5. I don't know who sent me the birthday card because I couldn't ___ the signature.

confiscate   6. The Russian communists, who opposed private wealth, ___(c)d the property of wealthy landowners.

qualm   7. Through the years, people with ___s about having cheated on their income taxes have sent gifts of money to the IRS.

retaliate   8. The Rumanian people ___(e)d against their communist dictator, who had ordered mass murders, by executing him.

benefactor   9. The high school's chief ___ has offered to pay all college costs for any low-income student who graduates from the school.

sinister   10. One of the oddest ___ plots of all time was thought up by a wealthy Frenchman. He fed his victims rich foods until they died of overeating.

scrutiny   11. Don't buy a used car unless you examine it closely and also have a mechanic give it careful ___.

rigor   12. Before the turn of the century, the ___s of prizefighting included boxing without gloves.

(Continues on next page)

PART B
Write **C** if the italicized word is used **correctly**. Write **I** if the word is used **incorrectly**.

_I_   13. Finally getting the raise she had hoped for *devastated* Jill.

_C_   14. A typewriter or word processor is *indispensable* for preparing a college term paper.

_C_   15. Since baldness is a masculine trait, why don't more men view it as attractively *virile?*

_I_   16. Because of the *recession*, retailers had an excellent year.

_C_   17. I don't consider retirement benefits a sufficient *incentive* to stick with a job I dislike.

_I_   18. All the newspapers reported the heroic deed of the *infamous* firefighters who rescued six children from a burning building.

_C_   19. The Democratic and Republican parties are *predominant* in the United States, but other parties are also represented on our ballots.

_I_   20. A wonderfully *incoherent* speaker, Abraham Lincoln was widely admired for his powerful speeches.

_C_   21. The desire to aid others seems *intrinsic* to many animals. Baboons, for example, will try to free other baboons who are caged.

_C_   22. Since my brother and I live next door to each other, we've *incorporated* our back yards into one big playground for our children.

_I_   23. In the *hypothetical* work of Dr. Martin Luther King, Jr., nonviolence was combined with aggressive action.

_C_   24. When our English teacher was fired because of his odd teaching practices, our entire class *interceded*, begging the school board to reconsider.

_C_   25. Farm *Sanctuary* offers a safe, comfortable home to farm animals who have been rescued from cruel conditions.

Score   (Number correct) _____ x 4 = _____%

Enter your score above and in the vocabulary performance chart on the inside back cover of the book.

UNIT TWO: *Test 3*

PART A: Synonyms
In the space provided, write the letter of the choice that is most nearly the **same** in meaning as the **boldfaced** word.

_b_	1. **sanctuary**	a) encouragement	b) shelter	c) requirement	d) decline
_d_	2. **covert**	a) necessary	b) slight	c) natural	d) secret
_c_	3. **benefactor**	a) villain	b) entertainer	c) helper	d) owner
_b_	4. **alleviate**	a) take	b) relieve	c) repay	d) build
_a_	5. **intermittent**	a) off-and-on	b) within	c) perfectly clean	d) complex
_b_	6. **digress**	a) be the parts of	b) turn aside	c) read	d) guess
_d_	7. **plagiarism**	a) correction	b) distaste	c) failure	d) stealing another's writings
_a_	8. **confiscate**	a) seize	b) interpret	c) make up	d) waste
_d_	9. **garble**	a) respond	b) pay back	c) relieve	d) scramble
_c_	10. **constitute**	a) seize	b) coexist	c) form	d) assume
_b_	11. **prerequisite**	a) cause	b) requirement	c) encouragement	d) difficulty
_b_	12. **speculate**	a) notice	b) theorize	c) give in to	d) combine
_d_	13. **default**	a) upset greatly	b) plan	c) aid	d) fail to do something required
_b_	14. **revulsion**	a) charm	b) disgust	c) encouragement	d) something that weakens
_a_	15. **decipher**	a) interpret	b) think up	c) relieve	d) turn aside
_c_	16. **retaliate**	a) follow	b) cut short	c) pay back	d) disappoint greatly
_d_	17. **nominal**	a) necessary	b) obvious	c) evil	d) slight
_a_	18. **qualm**	a) doubt of conscience	b) inspection	c) requirement	d) demand
_d_	19. **concurrent**	a) most noticeable	b) complicated	c) weak	d) existing together
_c_	20. **intrinsic**	a) manly	b) wicked	c) natural	d) open to injury
_d_	21. **recession**	a) vacation	b) requirement	c) delay	d) business decline
_c_	22. **intercede**	a) disappoint	b) give in	c) come between	d) delay
_a_	23. **scrutiny**	a) inspection	b) moral strength	c) destruction	d) neglect
_b_	24. **contrive**	a) continue	b) think up	c) cut short	d) believe
_c_	25. **rigor**	a) energy	b) purpose	c) difficulty	d) harm

(Continues on next page)

PART B: Antonyms
In the space provided, write the letter of the choice that is most nearly the **opposite** in meaning to the **boldfaced** word.

_c_ 26. **immaculate**   a) confused   b) good   c) filthy   d) slight

_b_ 27. **suffice**   a) plan   b) be not enough   c) be just right   d) give

_a_ 28. **blight**   a) benefit   b) peace   c) increase   d) friendliness

_d_ 29. **incentive**   a) improvement   b) mix-up   c) failure   d) discouragement

_a_ 30. **gloat**   a) express regret   b) misinterpret   c) forget   d) resist

_d_ 31. **degenerate**   a) command   b) give   c) try   d) improve

_d_ 32. **indispensable**   a) perfectly clean   b) large   c) protected   d) unnecessary

_b_ 33. **implausible**   a) common   b) believable   c) righteous   d) inspiring

_a_ 34. **predominant**   a) uncommon   b) complicated   c) strong   d) early

_c_ 35. **blatant**   a) serious   b) unnatural   c) unnoticeable   d) beneficial

_c_ 36. **intricate**   a) encouraging   b) at fault   c) simple   d) unsteady

_a_ 37. **devastate**   a) comfort   b) educate   c) admit   d) continue

_d_ 38. **infamous**   a) believable   b) young   c) alive   d) honorably famous

_b_ 39. **curtail**   a) improve   b) extend   c) admit   d) beautify

_c_ 40. **incoherent**   a) quiet   b) well-known   c) logical   d) friendly

_d_ 41. **virile**   a) homely   b) unnatural   c) graceful   d) feminine

_a_ 42. **succumb**   a) resist   b) attract   c) learn   d) delay

_a_ 43. **incorporate**   a) separate   b) do openly   c) add to   d) lose

_d_ 44. **vulnerable**   a) clear   b) right   c) complete   d) protected

_b_ 45. **sinister**   a) small   b) good   c) humorous   d) simple

_a_ 46. **hypothetical**   a) real   b) constant   c) separate   d) unnatural

_c_ 47. **gaunt**   a) optimistic   b) well   c) plump   d) short

_a_ 48. **squander**   a) use wisely   b) ignore   c) become confused   d) continue

_b_ 49. **cynic**   a) enemy   b) optimist   c) patient person   d) expert

_d_ 50. **demise**   a) failure   b) youth   c) conclusion   d) birth

Score   (Number correct) _____ x 2 = _____ %

Enter your score above and in the vocabulary performance chart on the inside back cover of the book.

UNIT TWO: Test 4

PART A

Complete each sentence in a way that clearly shows you understand the meaning of the **boldfaced** word. Take a minute to plan your answer before you write.

Example: As an **incentive** to work better, the company *gives bonuses to workers who show special effort*.

1. One of the more **infamous** people I've heard of is _____ *(Answers will vary.)* _____

   _____.

2. One sight that makes me feel **revulsion** is _____

   _____.

3. The reason the plan was **covert** was that _____

   _____.

4. When Carolyn saw her essay grade, she **gloated**, saying, "_____

   _____."

5. During the math class, the teacher **digressed** by _____

   _____.

6. My apartment is so **immaculate** that _____

   _____.

7. A good friend of mine was once **devastated** by _____

   _____.

8. The novel's main character is a **sinister** doctor who _____

   _____.

9. When my neighbor cut lilacs off my bush for her home, I **retaliated** by _____

   _____.

10. One **prerequisite** for getting married ought to be _____

    _____.

(Continues on next page)

PART B

After each **boldfaced** word are a *synonym* (a word that means the same as the boldfaced word), an *antonym* (a word that means the opposite of the boldfaced word), and a word that is neither. On the first answer line, write the letter of the word that is the synonym. On the second answer line, write the letter of the word that is the antonym.

Example: _c_ _b_ **nominal**	a. personal	b. enormous	c. slight
_b_ _a_ 11–12. **confiscate**	a. give	b. seize	c. combine
_a_ _b_ 13–14. **alleviate**	a. relieve	b. worsen	c. raise
_b_ _c_ 15–16. **intricate**	a. musical	b. complicated	c. simple
_a_ _c_ 17–18. **incorporate**	a. combine	b. resist	c. separate
_a_ _c_ 19–20. **indispensable**	a. essential	b. expensive	c. unnecessary

PART C

Use five of the following ten words in sentences. Make it clear that you know the meaning of the word you use. Feel free to use the past tense or plural form of a word.

a. **blight**	b. **curtail**	c. **decipher**	d. **implausible**	e. **predominant**
f. **qualm**	g. **sanctuary**	h. **speculate**	i. **virile**	j. **vulnerable**

21. _____ *(Answers will vary.)* _____

_____

22. _____

_____

23. _____

_____

24. _____

_____

25. _____

_____

Score   (Number correct) _____ x 4 = _____%

Enter your score above and in the vocabulary performance chart on the inside back cover of the book.

Unit Three

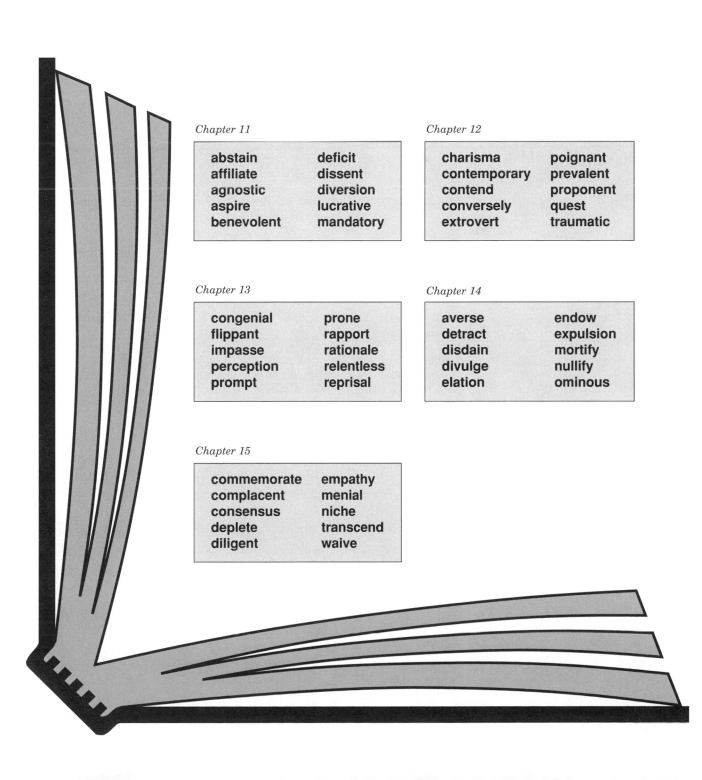

Chapter 11

abstain	deficit
affiliate	dissent
agnostic	diversion
aspire	lucrative
benevolent	mandatory

Chapter 12

charisma	poignant
contemporary	prevalent
contend	proponent
conversely	quest
extrovert	traumatic

Chapter 13

congenial	prone
flippant	rapport
impasse	rationale
perception	relentless
prompt	reprisal

Chapter 14

averse	endow
detract	expulsion
disdain	mortify
divulge	nullify
elation	ominous

Chapter 15

commemorate	empathy
complacent	menial
consensus	niche
deplete	transcend
diligent	waive

11

abstain	deficit
affiliate	dissent
agnostic	diversion
aspire	lucrative
benevolent	mandatory

Ten Words in Context

In the space provided, write the letter of the meaning closest to that of each **boldfaced** word. Use the context of the sentences to help you figure out each word's meaning.

1 abstain
(ăb-stān´)
-*verb*

- Although Lou has given up cigarettes, he doesn't **abstain** from tobacco. Now he chews it.
- My sister called off her engagement to Clayton because he wouldn't **abstain** from dating other women.

  c *Abstain from* means   a. to desire.   b. to believe in.   c. to deny oneself.

2 affiliate
(ə-fĭl´ē-āt´)
-*verb*

- Diane is neither a Democrat nor a Republican. She isn't **affiliated** with any political party.
- The young singer could have earned more if she had been **affiliated** with the musicians' union, but she couldn't afford the membership dues.

  a *Affiliate with* means   a. to join.   b. to study.   c. to hold back from.

3 agnostic
(ăg-nŏs´tĭk)
-*noun*

- Iris believes there is a God, and Marcia feels sure there isn't. Jean, an **agnostic**, feels that we can't be certain one way or the other.
- My uncle, who was an **agnostic**, used to say, "Humans cannot understand a flower, let alone whether or not there's a God."

  b *Agnostic* means   a. one who denies God's existence.   b. one who feels we can't know if God exists.   c. one who is sure there is a God.

4 aspire
(ə-spīr´)
-*verb*

- Twelve-year-old Derek, who loves drawing buildings, **aspires** to be a great architect.
- Millions of young people **aspire** to be professional athletes, but only a few will succeed.

  b *Aspire* means   a. to fear.   b. to wish.   c. to volunteer.

5 benevolent
(bə-nĕv´ə-lənt)
-*adjective*

- People are more **benevolent** when they get tax deductions for their donations.
- In 1878, William Booth founded a **benevolent** association to help the poor of London. He called it the Salvation Army.

  c *Benevolent* means   a. recreational.   b. profitable.   c. charitable.

6 deficit
(dĕf´ə-sĭt)
-*noun*

- The United States has spent so much more than it has taken in that it now has a huge budget **deficit**.
- Residents are asked not to water their lawns because a **deficit** of rain has dangerously lowered the water supply.

  a *Deficit* means   a. a lack.   b. an overflow.   c. a collection.

68

7 **dissent**
(dǐ-sěnt′)
-*noun*

• The committee was so torn by **dissent** that its members could not agree even on whether or not to schedule another meeting.
• The dictator permitted people to agree with his policies or keep silent about them, but not to express **dissent**.

_b_ *Dissent* means   a. plans.   b. opposition.   c. relief.

8 **diversion**
(də-vûr′zhən)
-*noun*

• My history teacher says that one of her favorite **diversions** during summer vacation is reading mystery novels.
• Skip likes his job, but he also enjoys such **diversions** as playing video games, watching baseball, and reading humorous stories.

_a_ *Diversion* means   a. a recreation.   b. something easy.   c. an assignment.

9 **lucrative**
(loō′krə-tǐv)
-*adjective*

• Investments in the stock market can be **lucrative**. However, they can also result in great financial loss.
• "Teaching at a small college isn't **lucrative**," Professor Baum admitted, "but I've never felt the need to make lots of money."

_b_ *Lucrative* means   a. required.   b. financially rewarding.   c. risky.

10 **mandatory**
(măn′də-tôr′ē)
-*adjective*

• Members of the basketball team have to follow strict rules. For example, it's **mandatory** that each player attend at least 80 percent of the practices.
• "A research paper isn't **mandatory**," the instructor said, "but if you write one, you'll get extra credit."

_c_ *Mandatory* means   a. unimportant.   b. helpful.   c. essential.

Matching Words with Definitions

Following are definitions of the ten words. Clearly write or print each word next to its definition. The sentences above and on the previous page will help you decide on the meaning of each word.

1. _aspire_   a. To strongly desire; to be ambitious (to do something or to get something)
2. _lucrative_   b. Profitable; well-paying
3. _deficit_   c. A shortage; a lack (in amount)
4. _abstain_   d. To hold oneself back from something; refrain
5. _benevolent_ e. Charitable
6. _agnostic_   f. A person who believes we cannot know whether or not there is a God
7. _mandatory_   g. Required
8. _diversion_   h. An amusement or pastime; anything that relaxes or amuses
9. _affiliate_   i. To associate; join
10. _dissent_   j. Disagreement

CAUTION: Do not go any further until you are sure the above answers are correct. Then you can use the definitions to help you in the following practices. Your goal is eventually to know the words well enough so that you don't need to check the definitions at all.

➤ *Sentence Check 1*

Using the answer line provided, complete each item below with the correct word from the box. Use each word once.

a. **abstain**	b. **affiliate**	c. **agnostic**	d. **aspire**	e. **benevolent**
f. **deficit**	g. **dissent**	h. **diversion**	i. **lucrative**	j. **mandatory**

_____*aspire*_____ 1. My kid brother ___s to become the video-game champion of the world.

_____*benevolent*_____ 2. The ___ fund at my church collects money to help poor families in our parish.

_____*diversion*_____ 3. My parents enjoy card games, but my sister and I like such ___s as computer games and music videos.

_____*mandatory*_____ 4. An entrance fee wasn't ___, but a sign at the museum entrance suggested that visitors make a donation.

_____*abstain*_____ 5. Because Hank needs to lose weight, his doctor recommended that he ___ from all sweets and fatty foods.

_____*deficit*_____ 6. We could overcome a(n) ___ of organs for transplants if more people would agree to have their organs donated after they die.

_____*dissent*_____ 7. There was no ___ in the family on whether or not to start a vegetable garden this year. We all agreed it was a great idea.

_____*affiliate*_____ 8. Yong could have joined the all-male club, but he prefers to ___ with organizations that welcome both men and women.

_____*agnostic*_____ 9. "When someone who believes in God marries someone who does not," the comic asked, "do they give birth to a(n) ___?"

_____*lucrative*_____ 10. Acting is ___ for only a small percentage of performers. The rest need additional sources of income, such as waiting on tables or driving a cab.

NOTE: Now check your answers to these questions by turning to page 128. Going over the answers carefully will help you prepare for the next two practices, for which answers are not given.

➤ *Sentence Check 2*

Using the answer lines provided, complete each item below with **two** words from the box. Use each word once.

_____*affiliate*_____
_____*diversion*_____ 1–2. My uncle decided to splurge and ___ with a country club because golf is his main ___.

_____*abstain*_____
_____*mandatory*_____ 3–4. Gale didn't ___ from smoking cigarettes at the office until her employer made not smoking ___. Keeping her job was a very good incentive° to get her to quit.

_____ agnostic _____   5–6. Some people think that since Stan is a(n) ___, he must be amoral°. It's
_____ benevolent _____   true he's not sure if God exists, but that doesn't mean he lacks a moral
                                   sense. In fact, he recently founded a ___ society at work to raise money
                                   for disabled children in the area.

_____ deficit _____   7–8. The ___ in the township treasury is causing a lot of ___ over whether or
_____ dissent _____   not taxes should be raised.

_____ aspire _____   9–10. Because my father ___s to make enough money to send his children to
_____ lucrative _____   college, he's working hard to make his auto repair business as ___ as
                                   possible.

➤ _Final Check:_ Conflict Over Holidays

Here is a final opportunity for you to strengthen your knowledge of the ten words. First read the following selection carefully. Then fill in each blank with a word from the box at the top of the previous page. (Context clues will help you figure out which word goes in which blank.) Use each word once.

While Jeanne and Paul are generally a happily married couple, they do struggle over one point of

(1)_____ dissent _____. They disagree as to how their family should observe religious holidays.

"The emphasis on presents," says Jeanne, "has made the season (2)_____ lucrative _____ for

all those mercenary° retailers who overcharge at holiday time. Also, people who should be watching

their expenses create unnecessary (3)_____ deficit _____s in their budgets by squandering°

money on unimportant gifts." She complains that exchanging presents at Christmas is practically

(4)_____ mandatory _____, whether or not one believes in the holiday's religious significance.

Jeanne (5)_____ aspire _____s to keep her home free of all such nonreligious customs

and thus wants her children to (6)_____ abstain _____ from traditions such as gift-giving

and dyeing Easter eggs. She feels the family's money would be better spent if it were donated to a

(7)_____ benevolent _____ organization for helping the poor. Some of Jeanne's neighbors assume

that she is a(n) (8)_____ agnostic _____ because of her lack of holiday spirit. They are wrong,

however. Jeanne believes deeply in God and is (9)_____ affiliate _____(e)d with a church.

While Paul understands Jeanne's concerns, he prefers the conventional° way of celebrating

holidays. "Children enjoy the customary (10)_____ diversion _____s that are connected with the

holidays," he says. "What would Christmas be without a visit to Santa and gifts under the tree? What

would Easter be without colorful eggs and an Easter egg hunt? These are pleasant practices that

enhance° the joy of the season."

Scores	Sentence Check 2 _____%	Final Check _____%

Enter your scores above and in the vocabulary performance chart on the inside back cover of the book.

CHAPTER

12

charisma	poignant
contemporary	prevalent
contend	proponent
conversely	quest
extrovert	traumatic

Ten Words in Context

In the space provided, write the letter of the meaning closest to that of each **boldfaced** word. Use the context of the sentences to help you figure out each word's meaning.

1 charisma
(kə-rĭz′mə)
-noun

- Kamal has such **charisma** that when he ran for class president, almost every person in the tenth grade voted for him. Such magnetism will benefit him throughout his life.

- Great Britain's Princess Diana obviously has great **charisma**. Despite her family problems, she still has numerous loyal fans worldwide.

_b_ *Charisma* means   a. feelings.   b. personal appeal.   c. luck.

2 contemporary
(kən-tĕm′pə-rĕr′ē)
-adjective

- Beth likes **contemporary** furniture, but her husband prefers antiques.

- My grandfather says that compared to kids in his day, **contemporary** youngsters are soft and lazy.

_c_ *Contemporary* means   a. common.   b. old-fashioned.   c. current.

3 contend
(kən-tĕnd′)
-verb

- The defense attorney **contended** that his client was insane and therefore could not be held responsible for the murder.

- Scientists **contend** that no two snowflakes are identical, but how could they possibly prove it?

_c_ *Contend* means   a. to wish.   b. to deny.   c. to declare.

4 conversely
(kən-vûrs′lē)
-adverb

- Ron, who is basically bored by food, eats in order to live. **Conversely**, Nate loves food so much that he seems to live in order to eat.

- Mary drives her children to school whenever it rains. **Conversely**, I make my kids walk because I think a little rain never hurt anyone.

_a_ *Conversely* means   a. in contrast.   b. in a modern way.   c. similarly.

5 extrovert
(ĕk′strə-vûrt′)
-noun

- Surprisingly, not all performers are **extroverts**. Offstage, many are quiet and shy.

- Ms. Stein hired Robert to greet and chat with her clients because he's such an **extrovert**.

_c_ *Extrovert* means   a. a supporter of causes.   b. a timid person.   c. a sociable person.

6 poignant
(poin′yənt)
-adjective

- The service honoring American soldiers missing in action was touching. A speech by a friend of one of the soldiers was particularly **poignant**.

- I cried when I read a **poignant** story about a dying girl who gave away all of her dolls to "poor children."

_a_ *Poignant* means   a. affecting the emotions.   b. correct.   c. lively.

7 prevalent
(prĕv'ə-lənt)
-*adjective*

- Unemployment was **prevalent** during America's Great Depression. By 1932, over twelve million people were out of work.

- Television sets are more **prevalent** in the United States than bathtubs. Over half of American homes have two or more TVs. Far fewer homes have more than one bathtub.

_b_ *Prevalent* means   a. favorable.   b. found frequently.   c. unlikely.

8 proponent
(prō-pō'nənt)
-*noun*

- I voted for Senator Williams, a **proponent** of improved services for the elderly, because I feel that many older people need greater assistance.

- Although Elaine quit work to take care of her children, she is a **proponent** of employer-supported day care.

_c_ *Proponent* means   a. a recipient.   b. an opponent.   c. a supporter.

9 quest
(kwĕst)
-*noun*

- During Carlo's **quest** for the perfect pizza, he sampled the cheese pizza at twenty-seven different restaurants.

- Ponce de Leon's **quest** was for the Fountain of Youth; what he found instead was Florida.

_a_ *Quest* means   a. a hunt.   b. a question.   c. design.

10 traumatic
(trô-măt'ĭk)
-*adjective*

- Divorce can be less **traumatic** for children if their fears and feelings are taken into account as the divorce takes place.

- My cousin has had nightmares ever since his **traumatic** experience of being trapped in a coal mine.

_c_ *Traumatic* means   a. familiar.   b. reasonable.   c. upsetting.

Matching Words with Definitions

Following are definitions of the ten words. Clearly write or print each word next to its definition. The sentences above and on the previous page will help you decide on the meaning of each word.

1. _____conversely_____   a. In an opposite manner; in an altogether different way

2. _____charisma_____   b. The quality of a leader which captures great popular devotion; personal magnetism; charm

3. _____quest_____   c. A search; pursuit

4. _____prevalent_____   d. Widespread; common

5. _____contend_____   e. To state to be so; claim; affirm

6. _____contemporary_____   f. Modern; up-to-date

7. _____proponent_____   g. Someone who supports a cause

8. _____poignant_____   h. Emotionally moving; touching

9. _____traumatic_____   i. Causing painful emotions, with possible long-lasting psychological effects

10. _____extrovert_____   j. An outgoing, sociable person

CAUTION: Do not go any further until you are sure the above answers are correct. Then you can use the definitions to help you in the following practices. Your goal is eventually to know the words well enough so that you don't need to check the definitions at all.

➤ *Sentence Check 1*

Using the answer line provided, complete each item below with the correct word from the box. Use each word once.

a. **charisma**	b. **contemporary**	c. **contend**	d. **conversely**	e. **extrovert**
f. **poignant**	g. **prevalent**	h. **proponent**	i. **quest**	j. **traumatic**

Conversely   1. I study best in the morning. ___, my sister concentrates better at night.

extrovert   2. Nancy is a(n) ___ by nature, but since she's become depressed, she has avoided other people.

poignant   3. At the airport, I was very moved by the ___ reunion of family members who had been separated for years.

prevalent   4. Underage drinking was so ___ in the fraternity house that college officials ordered the house closed for a year.

contend   5. "This woman ___s that she was here before you," said the supermarket checkout clerk. "Is it her turn now?"

proponent   6. Felipe is a(n) ___ of exercising for good health. He even encourages his young children to swim or cycle every day.

charisma   7. Certain movie stars may not be great actors, but they have a(n) ___ that makes people want to see their films.

contemporary   8. Abby didn't like the apartment with the old-fashioned tub and radiators. She preferred a more ___ place.

traumatic   9. Repeating third grade was ___ for my brother. It still pains him to think about it, even though he's a successful businessman now.

quest   10. Over the past three hundred years, several people have gone on a(n) ___ for Noah's ark. Some have looked for it in northeastern Turkey, on Mount Ararat, sixteen thousand feet above sea level.

NOTE: Now check your answers to these questions by turning to page 128. Going over the answers carefully will help you prepare for the next two practices, for which answers are not given.

➤ *Sentence Check 2*

Using the answer lines provided, complete each item below with **two** words from the box. Use each word once.

prevalent
contemporary   1–2. Many people are surprised to learn how ___ poverty is in ___ America. Today, millions live below the poverty line, and the number seems to escalate° daily.

extrovert
Conversely   3–4. Judy and Martin Reed exemplify° the old saying "Opposites attract." A(n) ___, Judy chooses work that brings her into constant contact with others. ___, Marty prefers jobs in which he mainly works alone.

_____traumatic_____   5–6. Ever since the ___ experience of finding her twelve-year-old son dead

_____proponent_____   from a drug overdose, Sophie has been a strong ___ of mandatory° drug education in the public schools. If drug education isn't required, she says, schools may cut corners and omit it.

_____contend_____   7–8. My mother ___s that _Romeo and Juliet_ is the most ___ story ever

_____poignant_____   written, but my sister claims _Love Story_ is more moving.

_____charisma_____   9–10. Mahatma Gandhi's ___ and vision inspired millions of fellow Indians to

_____quest_____   join him enthusiastically in the ___ for peaceful solutions to national problems. Gandhi incorporated° nonviolence and political activism into a highly effective method for social change: passive resistance.

➤ _Final Check:_ Dr. Martin Luther King, Jr.

Here is a final opportunity for you to strengthen your knowledge of the ten words. First read the following selection carefully. Then fill in each blank with a word from the box at the top of the previous page. (Context clues will help you figure out which word goes in which blank.) Use each word once.

(1)_____Contemporary_____ young people may be able to list the many accomplishments of the Reverend Dr. Martin Luther King, Jr. They may know that he was a civil rights leader who aspired° to achieve racial harmony and was a(n) (2)_____proponent_____ of peaceful but direct action. They may know that he fought the discrimination against blacks that was so (3)_____prevalent_____ in our country in the 1950s and 1960s. They may also know that he received a great deal of acclaim° for his work. For example, in 1964 he won the Nobel Peace Prize. They may even (4)_____contend_____ that he is the most important social reformer in the history of our nation.

But can the young really know the (5)_____charisma_____, the powerful personal magnetism of this man? He was a perfect blend of quiet, considerate thinker and bold, outspoken (6)_____extrovert_____. When Dr. King spoke, people listened. He had such a forceful yet (7)_____poignant_____ way of speaking that those who heard him felt his message deep within. For most, this meant a stronger belief in and respect for the man and his ideals. (8)_____Conversely_____, for bigots, it meant hatred and fear of what he stood for.

Dr. King's (9)_____quest_____ for equal rights for all was clear when he said, "I have a dream that this nation will rise up and live out the true meaning of its creed: 'We hold these truths to be self-evident; that all men are created equal.'" He gave his time, his leadership, and, in the end, his life. His murder was a(n) (10)_____traumatic_____ event in the lives of many Americans, who will never fully recover from that awful day. But because of Martin Luther King, Americans live with greater dignity. And many have taken up his fight for the betterment of all.

Scores	Sentence Check 2 _____%	Final Check _____%

Enter your scores above and in the vocabulary performance chart on the inside back cover of the book.

congenial	prone
flippant	rapport
impasse	rationale
perception	relentless
prompt	reprisal

Ten Words in Context

In the space provided, write the letter of the meaning closest to that of each **boldfaced** word. Use the context of the sentences to help you figure out each word's meaning.

1 **congenial**
(kən-jēn′yəl)
-*adjective*

- Our coworkers are very **congenial** except for Walter, who has remained distant and unfriendly toward everyone.
- I was nervous being at a party where I didn't know anyone, but the other guests were so **congenial** that I soon felt at ease.

c *Congenial* means

   a. persistent.
   b. intelligent.
   c. sociable.

2 **flippant**
(flĭp′ənt)
-*adjective*

- "Don't give me a **flippant** answer," George's father told him. "Your financial situation is a serious matter."
- When I told my son for the third time to clean his room, he gave this **flippant** response: "Why should I? I just cleaned it last month."

a *Flippant* means

   a. rude.
   b. serious.
   c. incorrect.

3 **impasse**
(ĭm′păs)
-*noun*

- The jurors had reached an **impasse**. They couldn't agree on a verdict— some thought the defendant was the murderer and others were sure he was innocent.
- If you think you've reached an **impasse** when trying to solve a problem, take a break. The solution may come to mind while you're doing something else.

a *Impasse* means

   a. a deadlock.
   b. a relationship.
   c. an opportunity.

4 **perception**
(pər-sĕp′shən)
-*noun*

- Brenda's **perceptions** of others are usually accurate. She is a good judge of character.
- Our **perceptions** of our problem differ. Rob thinks money is the main issue, but I believe it's a question of who controls the purse strings.

b *Perception* means

   a. a memory.
   b. a view.
   c. a desire.

5 **prompt**
(prŏmpt)
-*verb*

- To **prompt** Byron to get a job, I pinned the want ads to his pillow.
- Fast-food clerks **prompt** customers to buy more by asking such questions as "Would you like cookies or apple pie with that?"

c *Prompt* means

   a. to allow.
   b. to agree with.
   c. to motivate.

6 **prone**
(prōn)
-*adjective*

- Mr. Walker is **prone** to sleep problems, so he limits his intake of caffeine.
- **Prone** to fits of laughter during class, Chris sometimes controls the sound by biting into his pen.

a *Prone* means

   a. tending.
   b. immune.
   c. attracted.

7 rapport
(ră-pŏr′)
-noun

- In high school, I had such good **rapport** with my gym teacher that our close relationship continues to this day.
- If no **rapport** develops between you and your therapist after a month or two, start looking for a counselor who makes you feel comfortable.

_b_ *Rapport* means   a. report.   b. personal connection.   c. financial situation.

8 rationale
(răsh′ə-năl′)
-noun

- Danielle's **rationale** for majoring in business was simple. She said, "I want to make a lot of money."
- The **rationale** for not lowering the drinking age to 18 is that self-control and good judgment are not usually well developed at that age.

_b_ *Rationale* means   a. a situation.   b. a explanation.   c. a question.

9 relentless
(rĭ-lĕnt′lĭs)
-adjective

- The dog's **relentless** barking got on my nerves. He barked the entire two hours his owners were out.
- In a large city, the noise of crowds and heavy traffic is so **relentless** that it can be difficult to find peace and quiet.

_c_ *Relentless* means   a. occasional.   b. exciting.   c. nonstop.

10 reprisal
(rĭ-prī′zəl)
-noun

- In **reprisal** for being fired, a troubled man shot several people at the factory where he used to work.
- Fear of **reprisal** may keep a woman from pressing charges against a man who has abused her.

_b_ *Reprisal* means   a. disrespect.   b. revenge.   c. delay.

Matching Words with Definitions

Following are definitions of the ten words. Clearly write or print each word next to its definition. The sentences above and on the previous page will help you decide on the meaning of each word.

1. perception — a. Insight or understanding gained through observation; impression
2. prone — b. Having a tendency; inclined
3. relentless — c. Persistent; continuous
4. rationale — d. The underlying reasons for something; logical basis
5. flippant — e. Disrespectful and not serious enough
6. congenial — f. Agreeable or pleasant in character; friendly
7. prompt — g. To urge into action
8. reprisal — h. The paying back of one injury or bad deed with another
9. impasse — i. A situation with no way out; dead end
10. rapport — j. Relationship, especially one that is close, trusting, or sympathetic

CAUTION: Do not go any further until you are sure the above answers are correct. Then you can use the definitions to help you in the following practices. Your goal is eventually to know the words well enough so that you don't need to check the definitions at all.

➤ *Sentence Check 1*

Using the answer line provided, complete each item below with the correct word from the box. Use each word once.

a. **congenial**	b. **flippant**	c. **impasse**	d. **perception**	e. **prompt**
f. **prone**	g. **rapport**	h. **rationale**	i. **relentless**	j. **reprisal**

prone   1. Raquel is ___ to accidents, so her car insurance rates are quite high.

congenial   2. You will get along better in life if you are ___ to other people, rather than unpleasant.

flippant   3. My brother hides his lack of confidence by being ___. He rarely treats anything seriously.

prompt   4. It took his best friend's heart attack to ___ my dad to start exercising and eating right.

rapport   5. There was instant ___ between Duke and Otis. They talked as if they'd known each other for years.

impasse   6. At the movie's turning point, the bad guys reached a(n) ___. On one side of them was the police; on the other was a steep cliff.

relentless   7. During April and May, the rain was so ___ that we thought we might have to start building an ark.

perception   8. Floyd's ___ of human nature is strongly colored by some bad experiences. He thinks everyone is basically selfish.

reprisal   9. When Lacey and John divorced, she tried to get over half his income. In ___, he tried not to give her any of his income at all.

rationale   10. The ___ behind encouraging pregnant women to gain about twenty-five pounds is that low weight gain can lead to dangerously low birth weights.

NOTE: Now check your answers to these questions by turning to page 128. Going over the answers carefully will help you prepare for the next two practices, for which answers are not given.

➤ *Sentence Check 2*

Using the answer lines provided, complete each item below with **two** words from the box. Use each word once.

congenial
rapport   1–2. Because Wade is so ___ and easy to talk to, we established a warm ___ the first day we met.

rationale
prompt   3–4. Although the company president explained the ___ behind the pay cuts, his announcement ___(e)d an employee protest. However, once it was learned that the president was also taking a big pay cut, the employees' dissent° died down.

_____prone_____   5–6. My mother was ___ to anger and quick to punish me if I spoke to her in
_____flippant_____   what she thought was a ___ way. I avoided being with her any more
than necessary, so as not to risk eliciting° her rage.

_____perception_____   7–8. My ___ of the situation is that talks between the factory management
_____impasse_____   and union officials reached a(n) ___ because neither side would
compromise on salaries. In such situations, flexibility is a prerequisite°
to progress.

_____relentless_____   9–10. Abby could put up with occasional kidding, but her brother's teasing
_____reprisal_____   was often ___, going on for weeks at a time. Sick of it all, she finally
planned a(n) ___ that would embarrass him in front of his friends.

➤ *Final Check:* **Relating to Parents**

Here is a final opportunity for you to strengthen your knowledge of the ten words. First read the following selection carefully. Then fill in each blank with a word from the box at the top of the previous page. (Context clues will help you figure out which word goes in which blank.) Use each word once.

How do you respond when your parents deny you permission to do something? For example, if you want to travel and work around the country for the summer but your parents say you're too young, do you yell and demand that they stop curtailing° your rights? Do you plan a(n) (1)_____reprisal_____, vowing to spoil their summer plans because they've ruined yours? Or do you explain the (2)_____rationale_____ behind your request, so that your parents will understand your reasoning?

The way you behave when you and your parents reach a(n) (3)_____impasse_____ on an issue can have a big effect on how they view you. Sure, you could say, "Fine. Just fine. I'll go buy a leash so you can really run my life." But if you are consistently (4)_____flippant_____ like that, you'll just strengthen their (5)_____perception_____ of you as being too immature to be on your own. Also, if you are (6)_____relentless_____ in your begging, asking three hundred times a day, "But *why* won't you let me go?" they may tell you where to go, and it won't be on a cross-country trip.

Instead, approach your parents in a (7)_____congenial_____ way and try to develop a strong, friendly (8)_____rapport_____ with them. An amiable°, respectful relationship will make them more (9)_____prone_____ to see things your way. Even if you can't (10)_____prompt_____ them to change their minds about this summer's plans, your chances of getting their support will be better the next time you want to try something new.

Scores Sentence Check 2 _____%	Final Check _____%

Enter your scores above and in the vocabulary performance chart on the inside back cover of the book.

CHAPTER 14

averse	endow
detract	expulsion
disdain	mortify
divulge	nullify
elation	ominous

Ten Words in Context

In the space provided, write the letter of the meaning closest to that of each **boldfaced** word. Use the context of the sentences to help you figure out each word's meaning.

1 averse
(ə-vûrs´)
-adjective

- My son was once so **averse** to tomatoes that the very sight of them made him gag.
- Being **averse** to screaming crowds, I'd rather stay home and listen to my CD's than go to a rock concert.

_a_ *Averse* means   a. opposed.   b. accustomed.   c. open.

2 detract
(dĭ-trăkt´)
-verb

- Julius thinks the scar on his cheek **detracts** from his good looks, but it's barely noticeable.
- All of the litter in the park certainly **detracts** from the beauty of the trees and flowers.

_c_ *Detract* means   a. to result.   b. to benefit.   c. to take away.

3 disdain
(dĭs-dān´)
-noun

- The snobby waiter in the French restaurant viewed Tanya with **disdain** because she couldn't pronounce anything on the menu.
- I was afraid my request to see the state senator would be treated with **disdain**. Instead, the senator's secretary politely made an appointment for me.

_b_ *Disdain* means   a. pride.   b. disrespect.   c. sorrow.

4 divulge
(dĭ-vŭlj´)
-verb

- My father wouldn't **divulge** the type of car he had bought, saying only, "It's a surprise."
- It's against the law to ask people to **divulge** their age at a job interview.

_c_ *Divulge* means   a. to hide.   b. to recall.   c. to tell.

5 elation
(ĭ-lā´shən)
-noun

- The principal shouted with **elation** when the school team scored the winning touchdown.
- Roy had expected to feel **elation** at his graduation. Instead, he felt sadness at the thought of parting with some of his high school friends.

_c_ *Elation* means   a. anger.   b. confusion.   c. happiness.

6 endow
(ĕn-dou´)
-verb

- Nature has **endowed** hummingbirds with the ability to fly backward.
- Oscar Wilde was **endowed** with the ability to find humor in any situation. While dying, he said of the ugly wallpaper in his hotel room, "One of us had to go."

_a_ *Endow* means   a. to equip.   b. to curse.   c. to threaten.

7 expulsion
(ĕks-pŭl′shən)
-*noun*

- The manager told us we risked **expulsion** from the theater if we continued to talk during the movie.
- **Expulsion** from school is intended as a punishment, but some students may consider not being allowed to attend classes to be a reward.

_b_ *Expulsion* means   a. being canceled.   b. being forced out.   c. being embarrassed.

8 mortify
(môr′tə-fī′)
-*verb*

- It would **mortify** me if my voice were to crack during my choir solo.
- I doubt anything will ever **mortify** me more than the streamer of toilet paper that clung to my shoe as I returned from the ladies' room to rejoin my date in a fancy restaurant.

_a_ *Mortify* means   a. to shame.   b. to insult.   c. to delay.

9 nullify
(nŭl′ə-fī′)
-*verb*

- The college will **nullify** my student ID at the end of the term unless I update it with a new sticker.
- A soft drink company decided to **nullify** its contract with a well-known athlete because he was convicted of drunken driving.

_c_ *Nullify* means   a. to renew.   b. to reveal.   c. to cancel.

10 ominous
(ŏm′ə-nəs)
-*adjective*

- To many, cemeteries have an **ominous** quality, particularly at night or on Halloween, when the threat of ghosts can seem very real.
- The sore's failure to heal was **ominous**, a possible sign of cancer.

_b_ *Ominous* means   a. embarrassing.   b. threatening.   c. unworthy.

Matching Words with Definitions

Following are definitions of the ten words. Clearly write or print each word next to its definition. The sentences above and on the previous page will help you decide on the meaning of each word.

1. _____endow_____   To provide with a talent or quality

2. _____disdain_____   An attitude or feeling of contempt; scorn

3. _____expulsion_____   The act or condition of being forced to leave

4. _____ominous_____   Threatening harm or evil; menacing

5. _____divulge_____   To reveal; make known

6. _____averse_____   Having a feeling of dislike or distaste for something

7. _____mortify_____   To humiliate or embarrass

8. _____detract_____   To lessen what is admirable or worthwhile about something

9. _____elation_____   A feeling of great joy or pride

10. _____nullify_____   To make legally ineffective; cancel

CAUTION: Do not go any further until you are sure the above answers are correct. Then you can use the definitions to help you in the following practices. Your goal is eventually to know the words well enough so that you don't need to check the definitions at all.

➤ *Sentence Check 1*

Using the answer line provided, complete each item below with the correct word from the box. Use each word once.

a. **averse**	b. **detract**	c. **disdain**	d. **divulge**	e. **elation**
f. **endow**	g. **expulsion**	h. **mortified**	i. **nullified**	j. **ominous**

_____*detract*_____ 1. People talking in a movie theater greatly ___ from the enjoyment of watching a film.

_____*ominous*_____ 2. Because of the dark, ___ storm clouds, we canceled the softball game.

_____*averse*_____ 3. I'm ___ to speaking in public because I don't enjoy making a fool of myself.

_____*elation*_____ 4. When he received the college scholarship, my brother felt such ___ that he wept with joy.

_____*nullified*_____ 5. The results of the mayoral election were ___ after the townspeople found evidence of voting fraud.

_____*endow*_____ 6. The American water shrew is ___(e)d with feet that have air pockets, enabling the small animal to walk on water.

_____*expulsion*_____ 7. Some want a law calling for the ___ of illegal immigrants. Others want all immigrants to be allowed to stay in the United States.

_____*disdain*_____ 8. Vinnie's repeated boasts about his muscle-building backfired. They caused his date to look at him with ___, not admiration.

_____*divulge*_____ 9. Never trust Esta with a secret. She'll ___ it the minute you turn your back.

_____*mortified*_____ 10. The reporter was ___ when he learned that he had delivered much of his news story facing away from the operating TV camera.

NOTE: Now check your answers to these questions by turning to page 128. Going over the answers carefully will help you prepare for the next two practices, for which answers are not given.

➤ *Sentence Check 2*

Using the answer lines provided, complete each item below with **two** words from the box. Use each word once.

_____*averse*_____
_____*nullified*_____ 1–2. Some people are so ___ to living near a nuclear plant that they want the the plant's license to be ___. They say the plant threatens every homeowner's safety.

_____*endow*_____
_____*detract*_____ 3–4. Shannon is ___(e)d with beautiful curly red hair, but her self-image is so low that she feels her hair ___s from her looks. However, others find her hair to be one of her many attractive physical attributes°.

_____*divulge*_____
_____*expulsion*_____ 5–6. When someone ___(e)d to college officials that a certain student was selling drugs, an investigation began that led to that student's ___ from school.

_____mortified_____   7–8. Amy was ___ by the low grade she received for her class speech, a
_____disdain_____   grade she considered a sign of the teacher's ___ for her. However, the
teacher's rationale° for the grade was that the speech was incoherent°.
In addition to the lack of logic, it contained little solid information.

_____ominous_____   9–10. Marty had believed his headaches and blurred vision were ___ signs of
_____elation_____   some terrible syndrome°, so he felt ___ when he learned that he simply
needed glasses.

➤ *Final Check:* The Nightmare of Gym

Here is a final opportunity for you to strengthen your knowledge of the ten words. First read the following
selection carefully. Then fill in each blank with a word from the box at the top of the previous page.
(Context clues will help you figure out which word goes in which blank.) Use each word once.

I was not (1)_____endow_____(e)d with athletic ability. In a frequent nightmare,
I'm still trying to pass my mandatory° gym class so that I can graduate from high school. The
situation always looks grim. For one thing, the teacher has threatened me with
(2)_____expulsion_____ from school for refusing to take a group shower. Also appearing
in my dream is the terrifying vault horse, the very sight of which (3)_____detract_____s
from my mental health. I run toward the horse, leap, and nose-dive into the mat. Ignoring my
despair, the rest of the gym class laughs. Once again, I am (4)_____mortified_____ by my
athletic performance.

Next, a single (5)_____ominous_____ rope threatens overhead, where it hangs from the
ceiling. I try to contrive° some excuse to get out of climbing it. However, my excuses are so
incoherent° that my teacher says, "I don't understand anything you're saying. Get started."
Wondering if anyone has ever died from rope burn, I struggle to climb it. Almost to the top, I
sweat so much that I slide back to the floor, landing at the gym teacher's feet. "What a loser," the
teacher mutters with an expression of total (6)_____disdain_____.

Because I've always been (7)_____averse_____ to square-dancing, that too appears
in the nightmare. Having forgotten my sneakers, I'm forced to dance in my socks. I slip, rather
than dance, around the polished floor. During one high-speed turn, I go sliding—right into the
men's locker room, where the smell causes me to pass out.

The only pleasant part of the dream comes near the end. With amazement and
(8)_____elation_____, I learn that I will graduate after all. I smile, thinking I'll never
have to face the rigors° of gym class again.

But then, the principal (9)_____divulge_____s the terrible truth. I haven't managed
to pass gym. My graduation depends on my agreeing to take four more years of gym when I get to
college. If I don't, my high school diploma will be (10)_____nullified_____.

Scores   Sentence Check 2 _____%   Final Check _____%

Enter your scores above and in the vocabulary performance chart on the inside back cover of the book.

commemorate	empathy
complacent	menial
consensus	niche
deplete	transcend
diligent	waive

Ten Words in Context

In the space provided, write the letter of the meaning closest to that of each **boldfaced** word. Use the context of the sentences to help you figure out each word's meaning.

1 **commemorate**
(kə-mĕm′ə-rāt′)
-*verb*

- Thomas devoted himself to feeding the hungry. So on the anniversary of his death, it seems wrong to **commemorate** his life with a fancy dinner party that only the rich can attend.
- Each year, my parents **commemorate** their first date by having dinner at McDonalds, the place where they first met.

_b_ *Commemorate* means   a. to share.   b. to celebrate.   c. to believe.

2 **complacent**
(kəm-plā′sənt)
-*adjective*

- Elected officials cannot afford to be **complacent** about winning an election. Before long, they'll have to campaign again for the voters' support.
- Getting all A's hasn't made Ivy **complacent**. She continues to work hard at school.

_c_ *Complacent* means   a. very eager.   b. reasonable.   c. too much at ease.

3 **consensus**
(kən-sen′səs)
-*noun*

- A vote revealed strong agreement among the teachers. The **consensus** was that they would strike if the school board did not act quickly to raise their pay.
- The family **consensus** was that we should go camping again this summer. Ray was the only one who wanted to do something else for a change.

_a_ *Consensus* means   a. a majority view.   b. an unusual idea.   c. a question.

4 **deplete**
(dĭ-plēt′)
-*verb*

- I'd like to help you out with a loan, but unexpected car repairs have managed to **deplete** my bank account.
- In order not to **deplete** their small quantity of canned food, the shipwreck survivors searched the island for plants they could eat.

_a_ *Deplete* means   a. to use up.   b. to forget.   c. to find.

5 **diligent**
(dĭl′ə-jənt)
-*adjective*

- I wish I had been more **diligent** about practicing piano when I was younger. It would be nice to be able to play well now.
- Diane was lazy when she first joined the family business, but she became so **diligent** that she inspired others to work harder.

_c_ *Diligent* means   a. self-satisfied.   b. lucky.   c. hard-working.

6 **empathy**
(ĕm′pə-thē)
-*noun*

- Families who lost loved ones in the crash of TWA Flight 800 have **empathy** for one another because of their shared grief.
- Ms. Allan is an excellent career counselor partly because of her great **empathy**. She understands each student's feelings and point of view.

_b_ *Empathy* means   a. a common opinion.   b. a sympathetic understanding.   c. an efficiency.

7 menial
(mē′nē-əl)
-adjective

- Victor seems to think my summer job delivering pizza is **menial** work, but I've found that it requires some skills.
- Every job can be done with pride. Even **menial** jobs such as washing windows or scrubbing floors can be performed with care.

a Menial means   a. unskilled.   b. steady.   c. satisfying.

8 niche
(nĭch)
-noun

- Although her degree was in accounting, Laura decided her **niche** was really in business management, so she went back to school for more training.
- Dom spent the years after college moving restlessly from job to job, never finding a comfortable **niche** for himself.

b Niche means   a. a shared opinion.   b. a suitable place.   c. an education.

9 transcend
(trăn-sĕnd′)
-verb

- The psychic convinced her clients that she could **transcend** time and space and talk directly with the dead.
- Yoga can help one **transcend** the cares of the world and reach a state of relaxation.

b Transcend means   a. to participate in.   b. to go past.   c. to use up.

10 waive
(wāv)
-verb

- The defendant decided to **waive** his right to an attorney and, instead, speak for himself in court.
- Since Lin had studied so much math on her own, the school **waived** the requirement that she take high school algebra.

c Waive means   a. to lose.   b. to honor.   c. to give up.

Matching Words with Definitions

Following are definitions of the ten words. Clearly write or print each word next to its definition. The sentences above and on the previous page will help you decide on the meaning of each word.

1. _____*menial*_____   Not requiring special skills or higher intellectual abilities

2. _____*empathy*_____   The ability to share in someone else's feelings or thoughts

3. _____*transcend*_____   To rise above or go beyond the limits of; exceed

4. _____*commemorate*_____   To honor the memory of someone or something, as with a ceremony; celebrate; observe

5. _____*waive*_____   To willingly give up (as a claim, privilege, or right); do without

6. _____*consensus*_____   An opinion held by everyone (or almost everyone) involved

7. _____*complacent*_____   Self-satisfied; feeling too much satisfaction with oneself or one's accomplishments

8. _____*diligent*_____   Steady, determined, and careful in work

9. _____*niche*_____   An activity or situation especially suited to a person

10. _____*deplete*_____   To use up

CAUTION: Do not go any further until you are sure the above answers are correct. Then you can use the definitions to help you in the following practices. Your goal is eventually to know the words well enough so that you don't need to check the definitions at all.

➤ *Sentence Check 1*

Using the answer line provided, complete each item below with the correct word from the box. Use each word once.

a. **commemorate**	b. **complacent**	c. **consensus**	d. **deplete**	e. **diligent**
f. **empathy**	g. **menial**	h. **niche**	i. **transcend**	j. **waive**

_____*waive*_____ 1. The old man decided to ___ any claim he had to the family fortune, preferring to see the money go to the younger generation.

_____*commemorate*_____ 2. The American Inventors' Association gathered at a banquet to ___ Thomas Edison.

_____*deplete*_____ 3. My grandfather, who's recovering from heart surgery, is weak, so it doesn't take much effort for him to ___ the little energy he has.

_____*transcend*_____ 4. Many people believe that Shakespeare's works ___ those of all other authors.

_____*complacent*_____ 5. The restaurant got off to a good start, but then the owners became ___ about their success and stopped trying to attract new customers.

_____*niche*_____ 6. Several sessions with a career counselor helped Suzanne consider what her ___ in the working world might be.

_____*menial*_____ 7. The children help out at the family restaurant, but they are able to perform only ___ tasks such as mopping floors and cleaning tables.

_____*diligent*_____ 8. Arnie has been ___ in his study of German because he hopes to speak the language with his relatives from Germany when they visit next summer.

_____*consensus*_____ 9. I had hoped the restaurant would be good, but our group's ___ was that the food was only so-so and the service was even worse.

_____*empathy*_____ 10. Dr. Grange is a brilliant mathematician, but she lacks ___ for her students. She doesn't understand how they can find some problems so difficult.

NOTE: Now check your answers to these questions by turning to page 128. Going over the answers carefully will help you prepare for the next two practices, for which answers are not given.

➤ *Sentence Check 2*

Using the answer lines provided, complete each item below with **two** words from the box. Use each word once.

_____*waive*_____
_____*deplete*_____ 1–2. Lynn begged the bank to ___ the overdraft charge of thirty dollars, telling them that it would entirely ___ her savings.

_____*consensus*_____
_____*empathy*_____ 3–4. In high school, Victor was voted "Most Likely to Become a Psychologist." It was the ___ of his classmates that he was the student endowed° with the most ___ for other people.

_____*niche*_____
_____*transcend*_____ 5–6. My mother could have stayed in her comfortable ___ as part of the secretarial pool, but she wanted to ___ the limits of that job and become an executive herself.

_____commemorate_____
_____menial_____   7–8. "On this, our hundredth anniversary celebration," said the company president, "I'd like to ___ our founder with a toast. He ran the company from top to bottom, doing even such ___ jobs as emptying garbage cans. He truly exemplified° the values of dedication and hard work."

_____diligent_____
_____complacent_____   9–10. Dr. Roberts and Dr. Krill practice medicine very differently. Dr. Roberts is ___ about reading journals and learning new techniques. Conversely°, Dr. Krill is more ___ and never tries anything new.

➤ _Final Check:_ A Model Teacher

Here is a final opportunity for you to strengthen your knowledge of the ten words. First read the following selection carefully. Then fill in each blank with a word from the box at the top of the previous page. (Context clues will help you figure out which word goes in which blank.) Use each word once.

At Eastman High School reunions, the conversation usually gets around to the question "Who was the best teacher in school?" And year after year, the (1)_____consensus_____ of the graduates has been that Mr. MacDonald was the best. Many remember Joe MacDonald as the epitome° of teaching—the teacher against whom they measured all others.

He had started his professional life as a highly paid attorney. However, never at home with the law, he left his lucrative° practice and found his (2) _____niche_____ as an English teacher in the shabby classrooms at Eastman. Mr. MacDonald somehow helped his students (3)_____transcend_____ their broken-down surroundings and experience the magic in the words of Shakespeare, Dickinson, or Frost. Even those who tended to avoid reading began to think there might be something to this literature stuff after all.

Mr. MacDonald's enthusiasm for his work was never (4)_____deplete_____(e)d. In fact, instead of being used up, his enthusiasm actually increased through the years. Other teachers became (5)_____complacent_____ about their work and did very little lesson preparation. But Mr. MacDonald was as (6)_____diligent_____ as an eager first-year teacher. He could often be found talking with students after school, as his great (7)_____empathy_____ had given him the reputation of being someone who understood students' problems. He was fun, too. On the first really beautiful spring day of each year, he'd (8)_____waive_____ his lesson plan and take the class out into the sunshine to sit under the blue sky and talk about literature. And no task was too (9)_____menial_____ for him. He was often seen picking up trash from the grounds—something other teachers would never do.

After Mr. MacDonald's retirement, his former students wanted to honor him in some way. They thought about a statue, but decided to (10)_____commemorate_____ his teaching in the way that he'd like best, with a college scholarship for an Eastman student, which was established in his name.

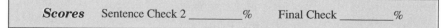

Scores	Sentence Check 2 _____%	Final Check _____%

Enter your scores above and in the vocabulary performance chart on the inside back cover of the book.

UNIT THREE: Review

The box at the right lists twenty-five words from Unit Three. Using the clues at the bottom of the page, fill in these words to complete the puzzle that follows.

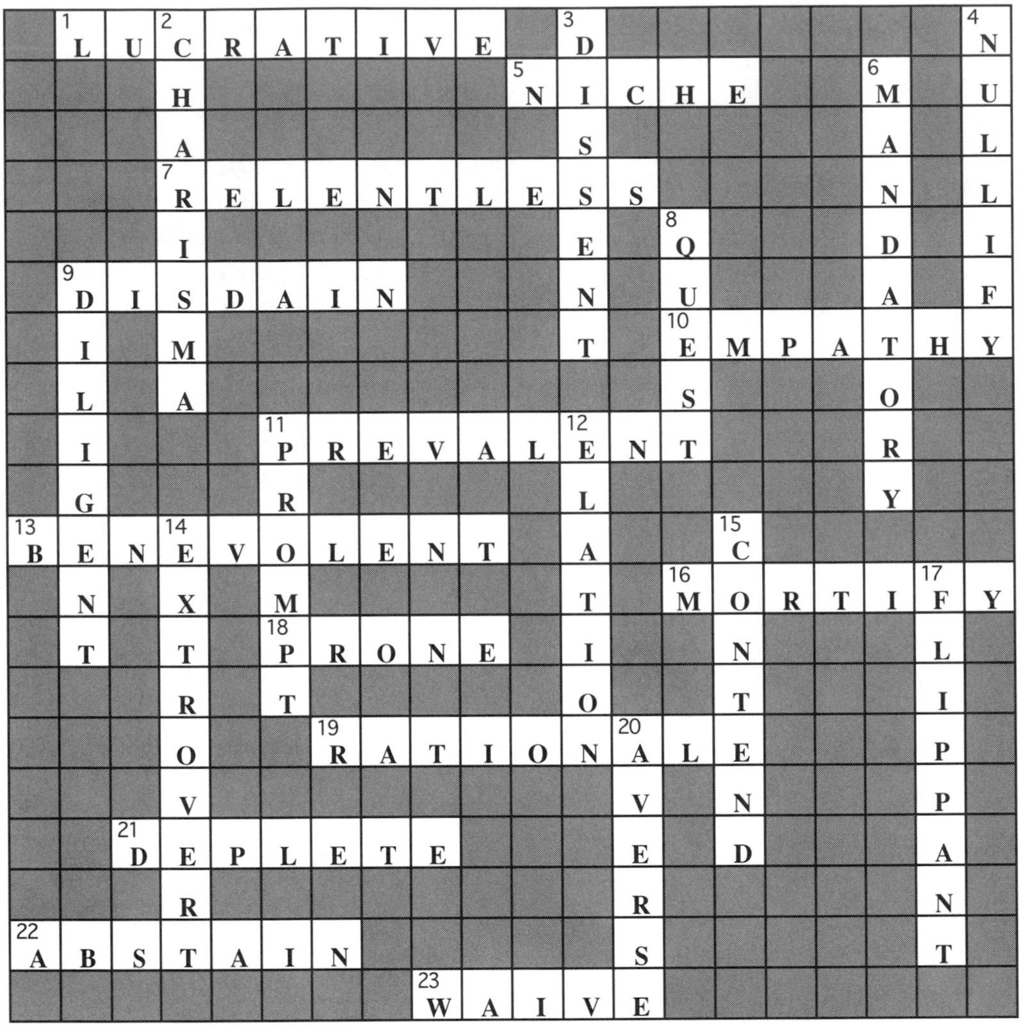

The crossword grid contains the following answers:

1. LUCRATIVE
5. NICHE
7. RELENTLESS
9. DISDAIN
10. EMPATHY
11. PREVALENT
13. BENEVOLENT
16. MORTIFY
18. PRONE
19. RATIONALE
21. DEPLETE
22. ABSTAIN
23. WAIVE

Word box:
abstain
averse
benevolent
charisma
contend
deplete
diligent
disdain
dissent
elation
empathy
extrovert
flippant
lucrative
mandatory
mortify
niche
nullify
prevalent
prompt
prone
quest
rationale
relentless
waive

ACROSS

1. Profitable; well-paying
5. An activity or situation especially suited to a person
7. Persistent; continuous
9. An attitude or feeling of contempt; scorn
10. The ability to share in someone else's feelings or thoughts
11. Widespread; common
13. Charitable
16. To humiliate or embarrass
18. Having a tendency; inclined
19. The underlying reasons for something; logical basis
21. To use up
22. To hold oneself back from something; refrain
23. To willingly give up (as a claim, privilege, or right); do without

DOWN

2. The quality of a leader which captures great popular devotion; personal magnetism; charm
3. Disagreement
4. To make legally ineffective; cancel
6. Required
8. A search; pursuit
9. Steady, determined, and careful in work
11. To urge into action
12. A feeling of great joy or pride
14. An outgoing, sociable person
15. To state to be so; claim; affirm
17. Disrespectful and not serious enough
20. Having a feeling of dislike or distaste for something

UNIT THREE: Test 1

PART A
Choose the word that best completes each item and write it in the space provided.

complacent   1. Admiring his build in the mirror, Lee gave himself a(n) ___ smile.

         a. ominous   b. complacent   c. agnostic   d. traumatic

ominous   2. My boss asked me into his office in such a(n) ___ tone that I was sure he was about to fire me.

         a. benevolent   b. congenial   c. ominous   d. prevalent

abstain   3. Alcohol is involved in nearly half of all traffic deaths in the United States, so people should ___ from drinking when they need to drive.

         a. divulge   b. abstain   c. endow   d. aspire

empathy   4. Keith is an excellent mental-health counselor who feels genuine ___ for those who come to him for help.

         a. elation   b. quest   c. empathy   d. niche

diligent   5. I'm not quick with home repairs, but I'm ___. I work steadily and carefully until I get the job done.

         a. diligent   b. complacent   c. contemporary   d. ominous

elation   6. When Scott won the gymnastics competition, his parents' ___ was as great as his own joy and pride.

         a. deficit   b. expulsion   c. elation   d. niche

Proponents   7. ___ of gun control point out that gun accidents in American homes result in over a thousand deaths each year.

         a. Quests   b. Agnostics   c. Proponents   d. Extroverts

impasse   8. The talks between the two countries reached a(n) ___ when each side claimed the oil-rich border area as its own.

         a. charisma   b. rapport   c. elation   d. impasse

Prone   9. ___ to oversleeping, Sherman keeps his alarm clock across the room so he has to get out of bed to turn it off.

         a. Flippant   b. Lucrative   c. Prone   d. Mandatory

deficit   10. When I realized that I didn't have enough money for holiday gifts, I decided to overcome the ___ by taking an extra part-time job in December.

         a. charisma   b. perception   c. dissent   d. deficit

(Continues on next page)

_____poignant_____ 11. It was ___ to see the bear immediately adopt the orphaned cub.

         a. flippant   b. poignant   c. relentless   d. lucrative

_____mortified_____ 12. Heather was ___ when, after diving into the pool, she bounced back up to the surface with the top of her bathing suit around her waist.

         a. nullified   b. mortified   c. adamant   d. ominous

PART B

Write **C** if the italicized word is used **correctly**. Write **I** if the word is used **incorrectly**.

_I_ 13. When I was a child, I hated broccoli, but now I'm quite *averse* to it.

_I_ 14. The *benevolent* boss laid workers off without even giving them a week's pay.

_C_ 15. "That bow tie *detracts* from Alan's appearance," said Paloma. "He looks strangled and gift-wrapped."

_I_ 16. Priests, rabbis, and other *agnostics* signed the petition asking for aid to the homeless.

_C_ 17. Eric has often had cats, but never dogs. *Conversely,* Joan has often had dogs, but never cats.

_C_ 18. A course in American history isn't *mandatory* at most colleges, but our school does require first-year students to take one.

_I_ 19. The company president was so impressed with Greta's sales record that he honored her with *expulsion*.

_C_ 20. My sister didn't find her career *niche* until she took a computer course and discovered her talent for programming.

_C_ 21. At the restaurant, Kevin *prompted* me to save room for dessert by saying, "They make the world's best chocolate layer cake here."

_I_ 22. Halloween has *contemporary* roots. Each year, the ancient Irish would dress as demons and witches to frighten away ghosts who might otherwise claim their bodies.

_C_ 23. The *relentless* beat of my neighbor's stereo gave me an equally persistent headache.

_I_ 24. After working in a hospital one summer, Andy has great *disdain* for the hard-working nurses he feels serve the patients so well.

_C_ 25. Because *menial* tasks require little thought, I was able to plan some of my essay while cleaning my apartment yesterday.

Score	(Number correct) _____	x 4 =	_____%

Enter your score above and in the vocabulary performance chart on the inside back cover of the book.

UNIT THREE: Test 2

PART A
Complete each item with a word from the box. Use each word once.

a. commemorate	b. consensus	c. deplete	d. divulge
e. extrovert	f. flippant	g. lucrative	h. prevalent
i. quest	j. rapport	k. rationale	l. reprisal

divulge 1. I think it's selfish of Dolly not to ___ the secret recipe for her wonderful salad dressing.

rapport 2. I have excellent ___ with my brother, but I haven't spoken to my sister for years.

extrovert 3. Rudy is such a(n) ___ that he makes friends with most of the customers at his beauty salon.

deplete 4. Some expensive household emergencies, such as a broken water heater, have managed to ___ my bank account.

rationale 5. My ___ for using cloth napkins is that they result in fewer trees being cut down to make paper napkins.

prevalent 6. With violent crime so ___, some newspaper reporters now wear bulletproof vests when they cover a story.

lucrative 7. Halloween is ___ for candy manufacturers. The holiday earns them about a billion dollars a year.

consensus 8. The ___ among the city's sportswriters is that Bridgewater High will win the basketball championship this year.

quest 9. In some fairy tales, the hero searches far and wide, on a(n) ___ for some precious object or missing person.

flippant 10. When the principal asked Randy why he had spilled milk on some girls in the lunchroom, his ___ response was "Because they were thirsty."

commemorate 11. On Presidents' Day, the nation ___s George Washington and Abraham Lincoln.

reprisal 12. When her brother kept taking her bike without asking, Meg's ___ was simply not to warn him that one of the tires was going flat.

(Continues on next page)

PART B
Write **C** if the italicized word is used **correctly**. Write **I** if the word is used **incorrectly**.

_C_ 13. Sharon is *endowed* with the gift of photographic memory.

_I_ 14. In a democracy, it's important for people to *waive* their right to vote.

_C_ 15. The TV contract will be *nullified* if the star misses any more rehearsals.

_I_ 16. Whenever it snowed, the *congenial* boy next door would throw tightly packed snowballs at me.

_C_ 17. Bob's near-fatal auto accident was so *traumatic* for him that, a year later, he still refuses to get inside a car.

_I_ 18. Kira *aspired* to go to the dentist, but her tooth hurt so badly that she had no choice.

_I_ 19. The candidate lost the TV debate partly because of his *charisma,* which included sweating and stammering.

_I_ 20. Wayne has *transcended* his usual good grades by failing three out of his four classes this semester.

_I_ 21. The student meeting went extremely smoothly. There was quite a bit of *dissent* to giving the retiring art teacher a set of fine oil paints.

_C_ 22. Fashion designers influence our *perceptions* of what is attractive. For example, who would have thought a few years ago that jeans filled with holes would be considered good-looking?

_C_ 23. Groucho Marx once joked that he wouldn't want to *affiliate* himself with any club that would accept him as a member.

_I_ 24. Vanessa's current *diversion* is as a night-shift clerk in a supermarket. She took the part-time job temporarily to pay off some bills.

_C_ 25. The street's residents *contend* that they complained for months about the huge pothole before the city government did anything about it.

Score (Number correct) _____ x 4 = _____%

UNIT THREE: Test 3

PART A: Synonyms
In the space provided, write the letter of the choice that is most nearly the **same** in meaning as the **boldfaced** word.

_d_	1. **traumatic**	a) noisy	b) dramatic	c) advanced	d) emotionally painful
_c_	2. **charisma**	a) generosity	b) health	c) charm	d) knowledge
_b_	3. **transcend**	a) cancel	b) exceed	c) happen	d) respond
_d_	4. **aspire**	a) join	b) follow	c) succeed	d) desire
_a_	5. **prone**	a) tending	b) menacing	c) talented	d) legally allowed
_d_	6. **quest**	a) sympathy	b) hope	c) proper place	d) search
_b_	7. **lucrative**	a) agreeable	b) profitable	c) common	d) expensive
_b_	8. **diligent**	a) self-satisfied	b) hard-working	c) modern	d) unlikely
_a_	9. **rapport**	a) relationship	b) explanation	c) search	d) logical basis
_c_	10. **impasse**	a) disadvantage	b) lack	c) dead end	d) meantime
_c_	11. **abstain**	a) join	b) use up	c) do without	d) long for
_a_	12. **divulge**	a) tell	b) exaggerate	c) go beyond	d) disagree
_d_	13. **niche**	a) comfort	b) assignment	c) search	d) suitable place
_a_	14. **empathy**	a) understanding	b) great pride	c) anger	d) amusement
_c_	15. **ominous**	a) angry	b) criminal	c) threatening	d) not religious
_b_	16. **endow**	a) rise above	b) provide	c) lessen	d) have
_d_	17. **prompt**	a) discourage	b) conceal	c) agree	d) move to action
_a_	18. **rationale**	a) reasons	b) disagreement	c) great joy	d) limits
_a_	19. **nullify**	a) cancel	b) avoid	c) reveal	d) oppose
_b_	20. **perception**	a) desire	b) impression	c) knowledge	d) perfection
_a_	21. **diversion**	a) amusement	b) support	c) pride	d) division
_c_	22. **poignant**	a) friendly	b) dangerous	c) touching	d) required
_c_	23. **relentless**	a) unwilling	b) angry	c) constant	d) in an opposite way
_d_	24. **reprisal**	a) report	b) disagreement	c) surprise	d) revenge
_a_	25. **menial**	a) lowly	b) uncaring	c) uncommon	d) manly

(Continues on next page)

PART B: Antonyms
In the space provided, write the letter of the choice that is most nearly the **opposite** in meaning to the **boldfaced** word.

_b_ 26. **elation**   a) illness   b) sadness   c) cruelty   d) escape

_a_ 27. **deficit**   a) excess   b) correctness   c) support   d) work

_b_ 28. **contemporary** a) popular   b) antique   c) uncommon   d) unimproved

_d_ 29. **deplete**   a) prefer   b) occur   c) lose   d) increase

_c_ 30. **agnostic**   a) doubter of God   b) loner   c) believer in God   d) prophet

_a_ 31. **benevolent**   a) cruel   b) unhappy   c) poor   d) conceited

_d_ 32. **extrovert**   a) opponent   b) worker   c) leader   d) shy person

_b_ 33. **averse**   a) effective   b) tending toward   c) doubting   d) done slowly

_a_ 34. **dissent**   a) agreement   b) pleasure   c) success   d) prediction

_d_ 35. **consensus**   a) full count   b) majority   c) impression   d) minority opinion

_c_ 36. **detract**   a) conclude   b) remember   c) add to   d) face

_b_ 37. **expulsion**   a) recognition   b) welcoming   c) payment   d) regret

_d_ 38. **congenial**   a) in doubt   b) far away   c) dissatisfied   d) disagreeable

_c_ 39. **prevalent**   a) incorrect   b) difficult   c) uncommon   d) unpopular

_a_ 40. **waive**   a) claim   b) forgive   c) go below   d) oppose

_a_ 41. **mandatory**   a) unnecessary   b) easy   c) welcome   d) unlikely

_b_ 42. **complacent**   a) different   b) self-doubting   c) uncomplicated   d) trustworthy

_c_ 43. **proponent**   a) newcomer   b) inner-directed person   c) opponent   d) voter

_d_ 44. **conversely**   a) expertly   b) boldly   c) late   d) in the same way

_d_ 45. **flippant**   a) silent   b) persistent   c) curious   d) respectful

_b_ 46. **affiliate**   a) agree   b) quit   c) recognize   d) join

_c_ 47. **contend**   a) conclude   b) depend   c) deny   d) discontinue

_d_ 48. **disdain**   a) good health   b) agreement   c) comfort   d) admiration

_a_ 49. **mortify**   a) make proud   b) hide   c) disappoint   d) agree with

_b_ 50. **commemorate** a) recall   b) dishonor   c) discourage   d) praise

Score   (Number correct) _____ x 2 = _____%

Enter your score above and in the vocabulary performance chart on the inside back cover of the book.

UNIT THREE: Test 4

PART A
Complete each sentence in a way that clearly shows you understand the meaning of the **boldfaced** word. Take a minute to plan your answer before you write.

Example: I **abstain** from _____*smoking because I don't want to get lung cancer*_____.

1. Luis showed his **elation** at the news by _____*(Answers will vary.)*_____

   _____.

2. I **aspire** to _____

   _____.

3. Jon, who is a **proponent** of daily exercise, advised me, "_____

   _____."

4. At our school, it is **mandatory** to _____

   _____.

5. At parties, my **extrovert** friend _____

   _____.

6. I find it **detracts** from a restaurant meal when _____

   _____.

7. Lamont is **averse** to city life because _____

   _____.

8. Our father told us how **traumatic** it was for him to _____

   _____.

9. My **rationale** for going to college is _____

   _____.

10. When asked by the restaurant owner to pay his bill, the young man's **flippant** reply was "_____

   _____."

(Continues on next page)

PART B

After each **boldfaced** word are a *synonym* (a word that means the same as the boldfaced word), an *antonym* (a word that means the opposite of the boldfaced word), and a word that is neither. On the first answer line, write the letter of the word that is the synonym. On the second answer line, write the letter of the word that is the antonym.

Example: _c_ _b_ **prevalent**	a. heavy	b. rare	c. common
_a_ _c_ 11–12. **contemporary**	a. modern	b. rapid	c. ancient
_a_ _b_ 13–14. **divulge**	a. reveal	b. conceal	c. defend
_c_ _a_ 15–16. **benevolent**	a. evil	b. gifted	c. kind
_b_ _c_ 17–18. **congenial**	a. clever	b. pleasant	c. disagreeable
_c_ _a_ 19–20. **diligent**	a. lazy	b. believable	c. hard-working

PART C

Use five of the following ten words in sentences. Make it clear that you know the meaning of the word you use. Feel free to use the past tense or plural form of a word.

a. **consensus**	b. **deplete**	c. **dissent**	d. **empathy**	e. **niche**
f. **perception**	g. **prone**	h. **quest**	i. **rapport**	j. **waive**

21. _____ *(Answers will vary.)* _____

_____

22. _____

_____

23. _____

_____

24. _____

_____

25. _____

_____

Score   (Number correct) _____ x 4 = _____%

Enter your score above and in the vocabulary performance chart on the inside back cover of the book.

Unit Four

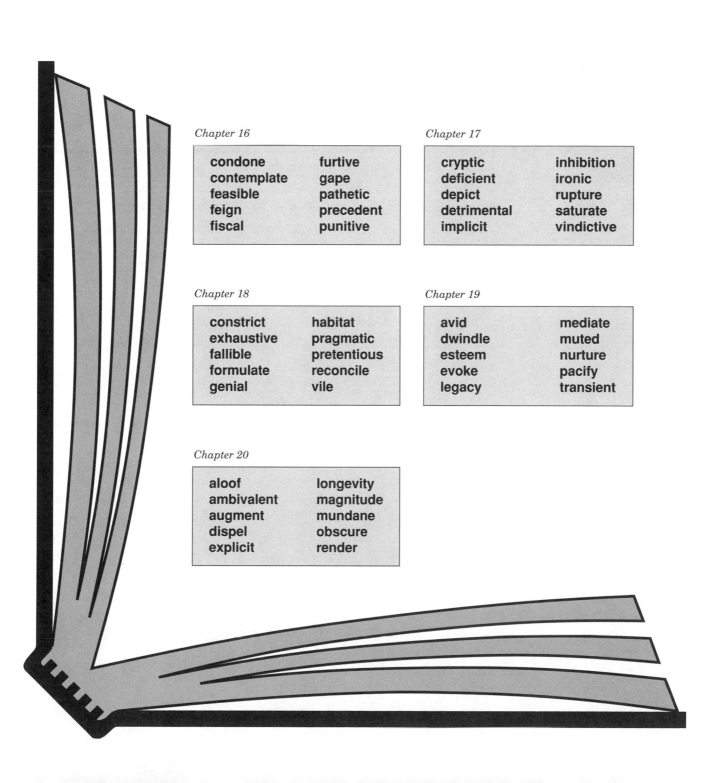

Chapter 16

condone	furtive
contemplate	gape
feasible	pathetic
feign	precedent
fiscal	punitive

Chapter 17

cryptic	inhibition
deficient	ironic
depict	rupture
detrimental	saturate
implicit	vindictive

Chapter 18

constrict	habitat
exhaustive	pragmatic
fallible	pretentious
formulate	reconcile
genial	vile

Chapter 19

avid	mediate
dwindle	muted
esteem	nurture
evoke	pacify
legacy	transient

Chapter 20

aloof	longevity
ambivalent	magnitude
augment	mundane
dispel	obscure
explicit	render

condone	furtive
contemplate	gape
feasible	pathetic
feign	precedent
fiscal	punitive

Ten Words in Context

In the space provided, write the letter of the meaning closest to that of each **boldfaced** word. Use the context of the sentences to help you figure out each word's meaning.

1 condone
(kən-dōn′)
-*verb*

- I cannot **condone** Barb's smoking in public It threatens other people's health.
- I can overlook it when you're five minutes late. But how can I **condone** your walking in to work an hour late?

a Condone means   a. to excuse.   b. to recall.   c. to punish.

2 contemplate
(kŏn′təm-plāt′)
-*verb*

- Because Ben hadn't studied for the test, he **contemplated** cheating. He quickly realized, however, that the eagle-eyed teacher would spot him.
- Whenever Anne's husband drank too much, she would **contemplate** divorce, but then she would feel guilty for thinking about leaving a sick man.

a Contemplate means   a. to consider.   b. to pretend.   c. to avoid.

3 feasible
(fē′zə-bəl)
-*adjective*

- It isn't **feasible** for me to work full time and keep the house clean unless my spouse shares the cleaning chores.
- Marilyn told her supervisor, "It just isn't **feasible** for this staff to do the work of the two people who were fired. You need to hire more people."

c Feasible means   a. wrong.   b. legal.   c. possible.

4 feign
(fān)
-*verb*

- Since I had heard about my surprise party, I had to **feign** shock when everyone yelled, "Surprise!"
- You can **feign** a head cold by pretending you're too stuffed up to pronounce an *l*, *n*, or *m*. Try it by saying, "I have a code id by dose."

c Feign means   a. to wish for.   b. to prove.   c. to fake.

5 fiscal
(fĭs′kəl)
-*adjective*

- The gift shop closed because of **fiscal** problems. It simply didn't make enough money to cover costs.
- Some states have passed laws allowing child-support payments to be taken directly from the paychecks of divorced parents who ignore their **fiscal** responsibility to their children.

b Fiscal means   a. emotional.   b. financial.   c. unfair.

6 furtive
(fûr′tĭv)
-*adjective*

- The detective noticed the **furtive** movement of the thief's hand toward a man's pocket.
- According to experts, teenagers who are **furtive** about where they are going and with whom may be involved with drugs.

a Furtive means   a. secret.   b. dependable.   c. serious.

7 gape
(gāp)
-verb

- Everyone stopped to **gape** at the odd-looking sculpture in front of the library.
- Because drivers slowed down to **gape** at an accident in the southbound lanes, northbound traffic was backed up for miles.

_c_ *Gape* means   a. to yell.   b. to appreciate.   c. to stare.

8 pathetic
(pə-thĕt′ĭk)
-adjective

- That plumber's work was **pathetic**. Not only does the faucet still drip, but now the pipe is leaking.
- Health care in some areas of the world is **pathetic**. People are dying of diseases that are easily treatable with modern medicine.

_b_ *Pathetic* means   a. ordinary.   b. miserable.   c. expensive.

9 precedent
(prĕs′ĭ-dĕnt)
-noun

- When Jean's employer gave her three months off after her baby was born, a **precedent** was set for any other woman in the firm who became pregnant.
- To set a **precedent**, the teacher gave the student who stole an exam an F for the entire course. "Others will think twice before they do the same," he explained.

_c_ *Precedent* means   a. a question.   b. a delay.   c. a model.

10 punitive
(pyōō′nĭ-tĭv)
-adjective

- Judge Starn is especially **punitive** with drunken drivers, giving every one of them a jail term.
- Many parents find that reward is a better basis for teaching children than **punitive** action is.

_a_ *Punitive* means   a. punishing.   b. forgiving.   c. uneven.

Matching Words with Definitions

Following are definitions of the ten words. Clearly write or print each word next to its definition. The sentences above and on the previous page will help you decide on the meaning of each word.

1. ____feasible____   Possible; able to be done

2. ____furtive____   Done or behaving so as not to be noticed; secret; sneaky

3. ____gape____   To stare in wonder or amazement, often with one's mouth wide open

4. ____precedent____   Anything that may serve as an example in dealing with later similar circumstances

5. ____condone____   To forgive or overlook

6. ____punitive____   Giving or involving punishment; punishing

7. ____fiscal____   Financial

8. ____contemplate____   To think about seriously

9. ____pathetic____   Pitifully inadequate or unsuccessful

10. ____feign____   To pretend; give a false show of

CAUTION: Do not go any further until you are sure the above answers are correct. Then you can use the definitions to help you in the following practices. Your goal is eventually to know the words well enough so that you don't need to check the definitions at all.

➤ Sentence Check 1

Using the answer line provided, complete each item below with the correct word from the box. Use each word once.

| a. **condone** | b. **contemplate** | c. **feasible** | d. **feign** | e. **fiscal** |
| f. **furtive** | g. **gape** | h. **pathetic** | i. **precedent** | j. **punitive** |

gape   1. Handicapped people don't like others to ___ at them. Instead of a stare, a simple smile would be appreciated.

contemplate   2. From time to time, I ___ attending business school, but so far I've made no firm decision.

precedent   3. Lawyers can strengthen a case by finding a useful ___ among previous similar cases.

feasible   4. It's not ___ for me to attend two weddings in the same afternoon, so I'll have to choose between them.

condone   5. The principal does not ___ hitting students. He believes that every problem has a nonviolent solution.

fiscal   6. At the low-cost clinic, Clayton had to give evidence of his ___ situation, such as a tax form or current pay stub, before he could receive treatment.

furtive   7. The people on the elevator didn't want to stare at the patch on my eye, but several took ___ glances.

pathetic   8. Mr. Hall's living conditions were ___. There was no heat or electricity in his apartment, and the walls were crumbling.

feign   9. When I gave my oral report in class, I tried to ___ confidence, but my shaking legs revealed my nervousness.

punitive   10. My mother wasn't usually ___, but one day I pushed her too far, and she said, "If you do that one more time, I will send you to your room for the rest of your adolescence."

NOTE: Now check your answers to these questions by turning to page 128. Going over the answers carefully will help you prepare for the next two practices, for which answers are not given.

➤ Sentence Check 2

Using the answer lines provided, complete each item below with **two** words from the box. Use each word once.

feasible
fiscal   1–2. "Would it be ___ for us to buy a new copy machine?" I asked at the office budget meeting. My boss replied, "Unfortunately, our ___ situation too tight. That purchase would create a deficit° in our budget."

punitive
contemplate   3–4. Some parents take only ___ measures when children misbehave. They never take time to ___ the benefits of a kinder approach. However, gentle encouragement is often more effective than punishment.

_____gape_____ 5–6. Several passersby stopped to ___ at the homeless man and his ___
_____pathetic_____ shelter, made of cardboard and a torn blanket. The poignant° sight moved one woman to go to a restaurant and buy a meal for the man.

_____condone_____ 7–8. The fourth-grade teacher said, "I will not ___ any ___ behavior in my
_____furtive_____ class. Rita, please read out loud the note you secretly passed to Ellen."

_____precedent_____ 9–10. The ___ was set many years ago: When the winner of a beauty contest
_____feign_____ is announced, the runner-up ___s happiness for the winner, despite the fact that she is quite unhappy at the moment.

➤ *Final Check:* **Shoplifter**

Here is a final opportunity for you to strengthen your knowledge of the ten words. First read the following selection carefully. Then fill in each blank with a word from the box at the top of the previous page. (Context clues will help you figure out which word goes in which blank.) Use each word once.

Valerie took a (1)_____furtive_____ glance around her. When it seemed that no one was watching, she stuffed a blue shirt into the bottom of her purse and darted out of the women's department. She walked slowly around the shoe department for a while and then left the store. "Stop! You! Stop!" shouted a guard who seemed to appear from nowhere. Then another man in street clothes grabbed her purse and pulled out the shirt.

"But . . . but . . . It's not mine. I don't know how it got there," Valerie cried.

The two men just looked at each other and laughed at the blatant° lie. The guard said, "That's what all shoplifters say. People steal without taking time to (2)_____contemplate_____ the possible results. Then when they're caught, they loudly (3)_____feign_____ innocence."

As the guard began to phone the police, Valerie pleaded with the men, "Please don't press charges. Please. This is the first time I've ever done anything like this, and I'll never do it again."

The men laughed again. "Your argument is (4)_____pathetic_____," the man in street clothes said. "It's everyone's first time. Our store has a policy on shoplifters: It's mandatory° for us to press charges, even if it's the first offense. We can't set a bad (5)_____precedent_____ by letting a shoplifter go, as if we (6)_____condone_____(e)d such crimes."

"That's right," said the guard. "Shoplifting is all too prevalent° in our store. This shirt costs only twenty dollars, but the twenties add up. Our (7)_____fiscal_____ officer has reported a loss of about $150,000 worth of merchandise to shoplifters last year. So it simply isn't (8)_____feasible_____ to let you walk away. Unfortunately, we have no choice but to take (9)_____punitive_____ action."

Soon Valerie was led to the police car. She covered her face as other shoppers stopped to (10)_____gape_____ at the lovely young woman, an unlikely-looking criminal.

Scores   Sentence Check 2 _____%   Final Check _____%

Enter your scores above and in the vocabulary performance chart on the inside back cover of the book.

cryptic	inhibition
deficient	ironic
depict	rupture
detrimental	saturate
implicit	vindictive

Ten Words in Context

In the space provided, write the letter of the meaning closest to that of each **boldfaced** word. Use the context of the sentences to help you figure out each word's meaning.

1 **cryptic**
(krĭp′tĭk)
-*adjective*

- I begged Tony to tell me the big secret, but he always gave the same **cryptic** reply: "It's a green world, my friend."
- Next to the dead woman's body was a **cryptic** note that said, "Not now."

_b_ *Cryptic* means   a. cruel.   b. mystifying.   c. humorous.

2 **deficient**
(dĭ-fĭsh′ənt)
-*adjective*

- When people have too little iron in their blood, it sometimes means that their diet is also **deficient** in iron.
- Gil's manners are **deficient**. For example, I've never heard him thank anyone for anything.

_a_ *Deficient* means   a. insufficient.   b. sensitive.   c. increasing.

3 **depict**
(dĭ-pĭkt′)
-*verb*

- The painting **depicts** a typical nineteenth-century summer day in the park.
- Harriet Beecher Stowe's novel *Uncle Tom's Cabin* **depicted** the cruelty of slavery so forcefully that the book helped to begin the Civil War.

_b_ *Depict* means   a. to hide.   b. to show.   c. to predict.

4 **detrimental**
(dĕ′trə-mĕn′təl)
-*adjective*

- Do you think all television is **detrimental** to children, or are some programs a positive influence on them?
- The gases from automobiles and factories have been so **detrimental** to the environment that some of the damage may be permanent.

_c_ *Detrimental* means   a. useful.   b. new.   c. damaging.

5 **implicit**
(ĭm-plĭs′ĭt)
-*adjective*

- When the gangster growled, "I'm sure you want your family to stay healthy," Harris understood the **implicit** threat.
- Although it's never been said, there's an **implicit** understanding that Carla will be promoted when Earl finally retires.

_c_ *Implicit* means   a. playful.   b. modern.   c. unspoken.

6 **inhibition**
(ĭn′hə-bĭsh′ən)
-*noun*

- A two-year-old has no **inhibitions** about running around naked.
- Sarah's family is openly affectionate, with no **inhibitions** about hugging or kissing in public.

_a_ *Inhibition* means   a. an inner block.   b. a habit.   c. a purpose.

7 ironic
(ī-rŏn′ĭk)
-adjective

- It's **ironic** that Loretta is such a strict mother, because she was certainly wild in her youth.
- "The Gift of the Magi" is a short story with an **ironic** twist: A woman sells her long hair to buy a chain for her husband's watch, while her husband sells his watch to buy ornaments for her hair.

a Ironic means   a. unexpected.   b. inadequate.   c. reasonable.

8 rupture
(rŭp′chər)
-verb

- If the dam were to **rupture**, the town would disappear under many feet of water.
- The bulge in the baby's stomach was caused by a muscle wall that **ruptured** and would have to be repaired.

c Rupture means   a. to heal.   b. to exist.   c. to come apart.

9 saturate
(săch′ə-rāt′)
-verb

- Most people like their cereal crunchy, but Teresa lets hers sit until the milk has **saturated** every piece.
- Studying history for three hours **saturated** my brain—I couldn't have absorbed one more bit of information.

c Saturate means   a. to protect.   b. to empty.   c. to fill.

10 vindictive
(vĭn-dĭk′tĭv)
-adjective

- If a woman refuses to date Leon, he becomes **vindictive**. One way he takes revenge is to insult the woman in public.
- After she was given two weeks' notice, the **vindictive** employee intentionally jumbled the company's files.

b Vindictive means   a. sympathetic.   b. spiteful.   c. puzzling.

Matching Words with Definitions

Following are definitions of the ten words. Clearly write or print each word next to its definition. The sentences above and on the previous page will help you decide on the meaning of each word.

1. _____inhibition_____   A holding back or blocking of some action, feeling, or thought

2. _____cryptic_____   Having a vague or hidden meaning; puzzling

3. _____implicit_____   Suggested but not directly expressed; unstated, but able to be understood

4. _____vindictive_____   Inclined to seek revenge; vengeful

5. _____depict_____   To represent in pictures or words; describe

6. _____rupture_____   To burst or break apart

7. _____deficient_____   Lacking something essential; inadequate

8. _____saturate_____   To soak or fill as much as possible

9. _____detrimental_____   Harmful

10. _____ironic_____   Opposite to what might be expected

CAUTION: Do not go any further until you are sure the above answers are correct. Then you can use the definitions to help you in the following practices. Your goal is eventually to know the words well enough so that you don't need to check the definitions at all.

➤ *Sentence Check 1*

Using the answer line provided, complete each item below with the correct word from the box. Use each word once.

a. **cryptic**	b. **deficient**	c. **depict**	d. **detrimental**	e. **implicit**
f. **inhibition**	g. **ironic**	h. **rupture**	i. **saturate**	j. **vindictive**

deficient   1. A person can be intelligent and yet be ___ in common sense.

rupture   2. When the pressure in the gas pipe became too great, the pipe ___(e)d.

ironic   3. Isn't it ___ that the richest man in town won the million-dollar lottery?

detrimental   4. Even something as healthful as vitamins can be ___ to your health when taken in very large amounts.

inhibition   5. Becky's customary lack of ___ was evident the day she came to class barefoot.

depict   6. In the novel *Oliver Twist*, Charles Dickens ___s life in an English orphanage as truly pitiful.

vindictive   7. Street gangs are ___. If anyone harms a member of a gang, the other members will take full revenge.

cryptic   8. The fifth-grade assignment was written in double talk. Everyone laughed as the students tried to make out the teacher's ___ message.

saturate   9. The aroma of Gretchen's perfume so ___(e)d the air in the car that Steve coughed and rolled down a window.

implicit   10. While it's not written in teachers' contracts, there is a(n) ___ understanding that teachers will spend time preparing lessons and responding to students' work.

NOTE: Now check your answers to these questions by turning to page 128. Going over the answers carefully will help you prepare for the next two practices, for which answers are not given.

➤ *Sentence Check 2*

Using the answer lines provided, complete each item below with **two** words from the box. Use each word once.

rupture
saturate   1–2. Water-balloon fights are fun until a balloon ___s against your clothes, and they get ___(e)d with cold water.

cryptic
depict   3–4. Most viewers find the painting, with its dozens of dots on a white background, to be ___. However, it's possible to figure out what the painting ___s by mentally connecting the dots.

vindictive
detrimental   5–6. I feel it's a waste of energy to retaliate° when someone has injured me, but my sister is always trying to get even with people. Her ___ attitude is ___ to her relationships with family and friends.

_____ironic_____   7–8. It's ___ that the book *Live Simply on Little Money* has made the author
_____implicit_____   wealthy, since a(n) ___ message of the book is that the author himself
                          requires little money.

_____inhibition_____   9–10. Gerry feels people should "lose their ___s" and do whatever they feel
_____deficient_____   like doing, but I think people who are altogether ___ in self-control
                          have poor manners.

➤ *Final Check:* A Nutty Newspaper Office

Here is a final opportunity for you to strengthen your knowledge of the ten words. First read the following selection carefully. Then fill in each blank with a word from the box at the top of the previous page. (Context clues will help you figure out which word goes in which blank.) Use each word once.

My therapist says it's (1)_____detrimental_____ to my mental health to keep my

thoughts bottled up inside of me, so I'll drop all (2)_____inhibition_____s and tell you

about the newspaper office where I work.

Let me describe my editor first. It's sort of (3)_____ironic_____ that Ed is in

communications because I've never met anyone harder to talk to. Alhough he's a proponent° of

clear expression, Ed communicates as unclearly as anyone I know. For example, if I say, "How are

you doing today, Ed?" he'll give me some (4)_____cryptic_____ response such as "The

tidal pools of time are catching up with me." I used to think there might be some deep wisdom

(5)_____implicit_____ in Ed's statements, but now I just think he's a little eccentric°.

Then there's Seymour, our sportswriter. Seymour is perfectly normal except that he has

unexplained fits of crying two or three times a week. In the middle of a conversation about the

baseball playoffs or the next heavyweight title fight, Seymour suddenly begins crying and

(6)_____saturate_____s handfuls of Kleenex with his tears.

Now, I don't mean to (7)_____depict_____ our office as a totally depressing place.

It is not entirely (8)_____deficient_____ in excitement, but even our excitement is a little

weird. It is usually provided by Jan, a (9)_____vindictive_____ typesetter who, whenever she

feels injured by Ed, takes revenge in some horrible but entertaining way. One of her favorite types

of reprisal° is sneaking fictional items about him into the society column. I'll never forget the time

Ed was in the hospital after his appendix (10)_____rupture_____(e)d. He almost broke

his stitches when he read that he was taking a vacation at a nudist colony.

Scores	Sentence Check 2 _____%	Final Check _____%

Enter your scores above and in the vocabulary performance chart on the inside back cover of the book.

constrict	habitat
exhaustive	pragmatic
fallible	pretentious
formulate	reconcile
genial	vile

Ten Words in Context

In the space provided, write the letter of the meaning closest to that of each **boldfaced** word. Use the context of the sentences to help you figure out each word's meaning.

1 **constrict**
(kən-strĭkt′)
-*verb*

• The summer highway construction will **constrict** traffic by confining it to only two lanes.
• For centuries in China, girls' feet were **constricted** with binding to keep them from growing to normal size. Women's feet were considered most attractive if they were under four inches long.

_c_ *Constrict* means   a. to expand.   b. to repair.   c. to squeeze.

2 **exhaustive**
(ĭg-zô′stĭv)
-*adjective*

• Don't buy a used car without putting it through an **exhaustive** inspection. Check every detail, from hood to trunk.
• My teacher recommended an **exhaustive** thousand-page biography of Freud, but who has time to read such a thorough account?

_b_ *Exhaustive* means   a. smooth.   b. detailed.   c. narrow.

3 **fallible**
(făl′ə-bəl)
-*adjective*

• "I know we all are **fallible**," the boss told his workers. "But do you have to make so many of your mistakes on company time?"
• When they are little, kids think their parents can do no wrong, but when they become teenagers, their parents suddenly seem **fallible**.

_c_ *Fallible* means   a. optimistic.   b. friendly.   c. imperfect.

4 **formulate**
(fôr′myə-lāt′)
-*verb*

• The author first **formulated** an outline of his plot and then began writing his mystery.
• Before stepping into his boss's office, Hank had carefully **formulated** his case for a raise.

_a_ *Formulate* means   a. to develop.   b. to question.   c. to accept.

5 **genial**
(jēn′yəl)
-*adjective*

• I was worried that my grandmother's treatment at the nursing home might be harsh, so I was relieved when the nurses and aides turned out to be very **genial**.
• Libby found her first dance instructor so harsh and unpleasant that she changed to a more **genial** one.

_c_ *Genial* means   a. good-looking.   b. practical.   c. good-natured.

6 **habitat**
(hăb′ĭ-tăt)
-*noun*

• Many people believe that wild animals should be allowed to remain in their natural **habitats** and not be captured and put in zoos.
• Mosses can live in a large variety of humid **habitats**, from very cold to very hot.

_c_ *Habitat* means   a. a pattern.   b. a plan.   c. a territory.

7 **pragmatic**
(prăg-măt′ĭk)
-adjective

- We always called my sister "Practical Polly" because she was the most **pragmatic** member of the family.
- When I was single, I spent most of my money on travel. Now that I have a family to support, I must spend my money in more **pragmatic** ways.

_a_ *Pragmatic* means   a. sensible.   b. patient.   c. pleasant.

8 **pretentious**
(prē-tĕn′shəs)
-adjective

- Dana's classmates don't like her because she's so **pretentious**. It's hard to like someone who acts as if she knows it all.
- My aunt marked her husband's grave with a large, **pretentious** monument, as though he were a member of a royal family.

_b_ *Pretentious* means   a. overly imaginative.   b. important-seeming.   c. cruel.

9 **reconcile**
(rĕk′ən-sīl′)
-verb

- When my grandfather died, we worked hard to **reconcile** Grandmother to the fact that he was really gone.
- After his third wreck in six months, Tony **reconciled** himself to living somewhere along a bus line and doing without a car.

_a_ *Reconcile to* means   a. to bring to accept.   b. to frighten about.   c. to hide from.

10 **vile**
(vīl)
-adjective

- My sister loves a certain cheese that has the **vile** odor of something that fell off a garbage truck.
- When I finally get around to cleaning out my refrigerator, I always find some **vile** moldy food at the back of a shelf.

_c_ *Vile* means   a. threatening.   b. natural.   c. nasty.

Matching Words with Definitions

Following are definitions of the ten words. Clearly write or print each word next to its definition. The sentences above and on the previous page will help you decide on the meaning of each word.

1. _____reconcile_____ To bring (oneself or someone else) to accept
2. _____habitat_____ The natural environment of an animal or plant
3. _____pretentious_____ Making a show of excellence or importance, especially when undeserved
4. _____fallible_____ Capable of making an error
5. _____constrict_____ To make smaller or narrower, as by squeezing or shrinking
6. _____exhaustive_____ Covering all possible details; complete; thorough
7. _____genial_____ Friendly, pleasant, and kindly
8. _____vile_____ Offensive to the senses, feelings, or thoughts; disgusting
9. _____formulate_____ To plan or express in an orderly way
10. _____pragmatic_____ Practical

CAUTION: Do not go any further until you are sure the above answers are correct. Then you can use the definitions to help you in the following practices. Your goal is eventually to know the words well enough so that you don't need to check the definitions at all.

➤ *Sentence Check 1*

Using the answer line provided, complete each item below with the correct word from the box. Use each word once.

a. **constrict**	b. **exhaustive**	c. **fallible**	d. **formulate**	e. **genial**
f. **habitat**	g. **pragmatic**	h. **pretentious**	i. **reconcile**	j. **vile**

vile	1. Our cafeteria serves the world's most ___ beef stew, full of big globs of fat.
genial	2. Why is Debra acting so unfriendly today? She's usually so ___.
reconcile	3. My mother was forced to ___ herself to my independence when I moved into my own apartment.
constrict	4. Bright light ___s the pupils of our eyes, letting in less light. Darkness makes them wider, letting in more light.
formulate	5. My supervisor told me that if I wished to work on an independent project, I should first ___ a detailed plan of my idea.
exhaustive	6. For her term paper on orchids, Wilma did ___ research, covering every aspect of the flower's growth and marketing.
Pretentious	7. ___ about his intelligence, Norm tries to impress people with a lot of big words.
habitat	8. Children's stories sometimes mistakenly show penguins at the North Pole. The birds' ___ is actually near the South Pole.
pragmatic	9. "It would be more ___," my daughter said, "if you went to the grocery once a week for a larger order rather than going daily for just a few items."
fallible	10. When the auto mechanic said, "Well, I'm ___ like everyone else," I responded, "Yes, but your mistake almost got me flattened by a truck."

NOTE: Now check your answers to these questions by turning to page 128. Going over the answers carefully will help you prepare for the next two practices, for which answers are not given.

➤ *Sentence Check 2*

Using the answer lines provided, complete each item below with **two** words from the box. Use each word once.

Reconcile / *fallible*	1–2. "You want me to be perfect, but that's impossible!" my daughter cried. "___ yourself to the fact that every one of us is ___." It wasn't until then that I realized how detrimental° my criticism had been to our relationship.
formulate / *habitat*	3–4. Wildlife experts ___(e)d a plan to preserve what little remains of the gorilla's natural ___. Continued loss of that territory would endanger the survival of the species.
pragmatic / *vile*	5–6. My roommate was not at all ___ about fiscal° matters. He would spend our household money on videotapes and ___-smelling cigars and leave us without food.

_____exhaustive_____   7–8. When our pet python escaped, we quickly made a(n) ___ search
_____constrict_____   throughout the house and grounds. We found him wrapped around our
                                       dog, about to ___ the poor mutt to death.

_____genial_____   9–10. At the sales seminar, we were taught to be ___ with customers and
_____pretentious_____   never to be ___, no matter how much we know. Customers like warm,
                                       amiable° salespeople, not ones who show off.

➤ *Final Check:* Roughing It

Here is a final opportunity for you to strengthen your knowledge of the ten words. First read the following selection carefully. Then fill in each blank with a word from the box at the top of the previous page. (Context clues will help you figure out which word goes in which blank.) Use each word once.

"Whose brilliant idea was this anyway?" Sara asked. "If people were intended to sleep on the ground and cook over a fire, we wouldn't have beds and microwave ovens."

"Stop complaining," Emily said. "At least *you've* got on dry clothes. You didn't end up walking through some (1)_____vile_____ mud because your canoe overturned. And you didn't have a (2)_____pretentious_____ partner who claimed to know everything about canoeing but actually didn't know enough to steer around a rock."

"So I made a mistake," George said. "We're all (3)_____fallible_____."

"Well," Emily responded, "your mistake has lost us our tent. And our sleeping bags and clothes are saturated° with muddy water."

Then Doug spoke up. "It's no big deal. Sara and I will lend you clothes, and you two can squeeze into our tent."

"Squeeze is right, " said Emily. "Four in one tent will (4)_____constrict_____ us so much that we won't be able to exhale."

"It's your choice," said Doug. "Decide if you want to be in a crowded tent or sleep out in this wild-animal (5)_____habitat_____."

Sara couldn't resist adding, "If you had listened to me and were more (6)_____pragmatic_____ when planning for this trip, we wouldn't be in such a mess. You would have written a(n) (7)_____exhaustive_____ list of what we would need, from A to Z. Then you would have (8)_____formulate_____(e)d a clear plan for who would take what. Then we wouldn't be out here with two corkscrews but no plastic to wrap our belongings in."

"Let's just stop complaining before this degenerates° into a shouting match. We should be a little more (9)_____genial_____ with one another," said Doug. "We need to (10)_____reconcile_____ ourselves to our imperfect situation and not let it detract° so much from our vacation that we forget to have a good time."

Scores	Sentence Check 2 _____ %	Final Check _____ %

Enter your scores above and in the vocabulary performance chart on the inside back cover of the book.

avid	mediate
dwindle	muted
esteem	nurture
evoke	pacify
legacy	transient

Ten Words in Context

In the space provided, write the letter of the meaning closest to that of each **boldfaced** word. Use the context of the sentences to help you figure out each word's meaning.

1 avid
(ăv′ĭd)
-*adjective*

- Ramia, an **avid** reader, enjoys nothing more than a good science-fiction novel.
- Artie is such an **avid** sports fan that he has two televisions tuned to different sporting events so he doesn't miss any action.

_b_ *Avid* means   a. likable.   b. devoted.   c. helpful.

2 dwindle
(dwĭn′dəl)
-*verb*

- As the number of leaves on the tree **dwindled**, the number on the ground increased.
- Chewing nicotine gum helped Doreen's craving for cigarettes to **dwindle**. She smoked fewer and fewer cigarettes each day until she quit altogether.

_c_ *Dwindle* means   a. to make sense.   b. to drop suddenly.   c. to decrease.

3 esteem
(ĕ-stēm′)
-*noun*

- When Mr. Bauer retired after coaching basketball for thirty years, his admiring students gave him a gold whistle as a sign of their **esteem**.
- The critics had such **esteem** for the play that they voted it "Best Drama of the Year."

_b_ *Esteem* means   a. concern.   b. appreciation.   c. curiosity.

4 evoke
(ē-vōk′)
-*verb*

- Strangely enough, seeing my son's high-school graduation picture **evoked** memories of his infancy.
- The smells of cider and pumpkin pie **evoke** thoughts of autumn.

_a_ *Evoke* means   a. to bring out.   b. to shelter.   c. to follow.

5 legacy
(lĕg′ə-sē)
-*noun*

- Ana's great-grandfather, grandmother, and mother were all musicians. She must have inherited their **legacy** of musical talent because she's an excellent piano and guitar player.
- One of the richest **legacies** that my mother handed down to me is the love of nature. I've inherited her interests in growing flowers and in hiking.

_c_ *Legacy* means   a. memory.   b. high hope.   c. inherited gift.

6 mediate
(mē′dē-āt′)
-*verb*

- My father refused to **mediate** quarrels between my sister and me. He would say, "Settle your own fights."
- Each of the farmers claimed the stream was part of his property. Finally, they agreed to let the town council **mediate** their conflict.

_b_ *Mediate* means   a. to participate in.   b. to settle.   c. to observe.

7 **muted**
(myoo**'**təd)
-*adjective*

- When I put in my earplugs, the yelling from the next apartment becomes **muted** enough so that it no longer disturbs me.
- The artist used **muted** rather than bright colors, giving the painting a quiet, peaceful tone.

a Muted means   a. soft.   b. temporary.   c. boring.

8 **nurture**
(nûr**'**chər)
-*verb*

- Although I often forget to water or feed my plants, my sister carefully **nurtures** her many ferns and violets.
- Many animals feed and protect their babies, but female fish, in general, do not **nurture** their young. The female only lays the eggs, which are guarded by the male until they hatch.

c Nurture means   a. to inspect.   b. to seek out.   c. to care for.

9 **pacify**
(păs**'**ə-fī**'**)
-*verb*

- When I'm feeling nervous or upset, I often **pacify** myself with a soothing cup of mint tea.
- Not only did I anger Roberta by calling her boyfriend "a creep," but I failed to **pacify** her with my note of apology: "I'm sorry I called Mel a creep. It's not always wise to tell the truth."

c Pacify means   a. to amuse.   b. to encourage.   c. to soothe.

10 **transient**
(trăn**'**shənt)
-*adjective*

- The drug's dangers include both permanent brain damage and **transient** side effects, such as temporarily blurred vision.
- Julie wants a lasting relationship, but Carlos seems interested in only a **transient** one.

b Transient means   a. dull.   b. short-lived.   c. hard to notice.

Matching Words with Definitions

Following are definitions of the ten words. Clearly write or print each word next to its definition. The sentences above and on the previous page will help you decide on the meaning of each word.

1.	*muted*	Softened; toned down; made less intense
2.	*transient*	Temporary; passing soon or quickly
3.	*avid*	Enthusiastic and devoted
4.	*pacify*	To make calm or peaceful
5.	*evoke*	To draw forth, as a mental image or a feeling
6.	*dwindle*	To gradually lessen or shrink
7.	*mediate*	To settle (a conflict) by acting as a go-between
8.	*esteem*	High regard; respect; favorable opinion
9.	*nurture*	To promote development by providing nourishment, support, and protection
10.	*legacy*	Something handed down from people who have come before

CAUTION: Do not go any further until you are sure the above answers are correct. Then you can use the definitions to help you in the following practices. Your goal is eventually to know the words well enough so that you don't need to check the definitions at all.

➤ Sentence Check 1

Using the answer line provided, complete each item below with the correct word from the box. Use each word once.

a. **avid**	b. **dwindle**	c. **esteem**	d. **evoke**	e. **legacy**
f. **mediate**	g. **muted**	h. **nurture**	i. **pacify**	j. **transient**

pacify   1. When my newborn nephew starts to scream, we ___ him by rocking him and singing softly.

evoke   2. The photos in my album ___ many fond memories of my high-school friends.

dwindle   3. If you study too long at one sitting, your concentration will eventually begin to ___.

muted   4. At the party, Yoko and I kept our conversation ___ so that no one would overhear us.

nurture   5. You must ___ a child with love and respect as well as with food and shelter.

transient   6. Part of the charm of spring is that it's ___. It comes and goes so quickly that I can't wait for its return.

esteem   7. To show his ___ for her singing, the talent agent sent Mary flowers after she performed in a local theater.

avid   8. My cousin Bobby is the most ___ collector I know. He collects almost anything, from baseball cards to beer cans.

legacy   9. Shakespeare's work, a priceless ___ from the sixteenth and seventeenth centuries, has been enjoyed by generation after generation.

mediate   10. Rather than go to court, Mr. Hillman and the owner of the gas station agreed to have a lawyer ___ their disagreement.

NOTE: Now check your answers to these questions by turning to page 128. Going over the answers carefully will help you prepare for the next two practices, for which answers are not given.

➤ Sentence Check 2

Using the answer lines provided, complete each item below with **two** words from the box. Use each word once.

esteem
transient   1–2. Becky's ___ for Gerald turned out to be ___. She discovered that he used drugs and could not condone° his habit, so she broke up with him.

avid
dwindle   3–4. Leo is such a(n) ___ chef that his enthusiasm for cooking never ___s. He's been known to cook for ten straight hours.

muted
pacify   5–6. Loud music upsets our canary, but ___ tones ___ her.

_____nurture_____ 7–8. It is necessary to ___ a human infant because it is the biological ___ of
_____legacy_____   newborn mammals to be unable to survive on their own. Parental care
                             is indispensable°.

_____mediate_____ 9–10. In the Bible, King Solomon ___s a dispute between two women, each
_____evoke_____   of whom claims the same child as her own. Pretending that the child
                             will be cut in two, he sees the horror that this thought ___s in one of
                             the women. He then knows that she is the true mother.

➤ *Final Check:* Getting Scared

Here is a final opportunity for you to strengthen your knowledge of the ten words. First read the following selection carefully. Then fill in each blank with a word from the box at the top of the previous page. (Context clues will help you figure out which word goes in which blank.) Use each word once.

Do you remember trying to scare yourself and everybody else when you were a kid? For instance, maybe you were a(n) (1)_____*avid*_____ roller-coaster rider, closing your eyes and screaming and loving it all. Afterward, you would (2)_____*pacify*_____ your still nervous stomach by quietly sipping an ice-cold Coke. If a short roller-coaster ride gave you too (3)_____*transient*_____ a thrill, there was always the long-term fear of a horror movie. If the horrors it depicted° were vile° enough, you might be scared about going to bed for the next three months.

And remember popping out from behind corners yelling "Boo!" at your brother? The fight that followed ("You didn't scare me one bit." "Did too." "Did not." "Did too.") would go on until a grown-up (4)_____*mediate*_____(e)d the conflict. (Parents always seemed to be there to settle disputes or to (5)_____*nurture*_____ and reassure you at times when you needed support.)

At other times, you and your friends probably sat around a campfire late at night, engaging in your favorite nocturnal° activity—telling ghost stories. Thrilled with the horror of it all, you spoke in voices so (6)_____*muted*_____ they were almost whispers. The storyteller who gained the most (7)_____*esteem*_____ was the one who could (8)_____*evoke*_____ the greatest terror in others. If anybody's fear started to (9)_____*dwindle*_____, this expert would quickly build it up again with the chilling story of the ghost in the outhouse, a (10)_____*legacy*_____ handed down from older brothers and sisters to younger ones. The story always made you so scared that you needed to go to the outhouse. But fearing the ghost there, how could you?

Scores   Sentence Check 2 _____%   Final Check _____%

Enter your scores above and in the vocabulary performance chart on the inside back cover of the book.

aloof	longevity
ambivalent	magnitude
augment	mundane
dispel	obscure
explicit	render

Ten Words in Context

In the space provided, write the letter of the meaning closest to that of each **boldfaced** word. Use the context of the sentences to help you figure out each word's meaning.

1 **aloof**
(ə-lōof′)
-*adjective*

- Some people say that the English are **aloof**, but the English people I've met seem warm and open.
- I knew that Taylor was upset with me about something because he was **aloof** even when I tried to be friendly.

c *Aloof* means   a. motivated.   b. lazy.   c. cold.

2 **ambivalent**
(ăm-bĭv′ə-lənt)
-*adjective*

- "Because I'm **ambivalent** about marriage," Earl said, "I keep swinging back and forth between wanting to set the date and wanting to break off my engagement."
- I'm **ambivalent** about my mother-in-law. I appreciate her desire to be helpful, but I dislike her efforts to run our lives.

b *Ambivalent* means   a. meaning well.   b. having mixed feelings.   c. experienced.

3 **augment**
(ôg-mĕnt′)
-*verb*

- Why are women willing to **augment** their height when high heels harm their feet so much?
- Because Jenna needed additional money, she **augmented** her salary by typing term papers for college students.

a *Augment* means   a. to add to.   b. to risk.   c. to cover up.

4 **dispel**
(dĭ-spĕl′)
-*verb*

- Vickie's sweet note of apology was enough to **dispel** the slight anger Rex still felt toward her.
- I tried to **dispel** my friend's fears about her blind date that evening by telling her that my parents met on a blind date.

b *Dispel* means   a. to cause.   b. to eliminate.   c. to communicate.

5 **explicit**
(ĕks-plĭs′ĭt)
-*adjective*

- The novel's sex scene was **explicit**, leaving nothing to the imagination.
- My parents were very **explicit** about what I could and could not do during their three-day absence. They presented me with a detailed list!

c *Explicit* means   a. brief.   b. mysterious.   c. specific.

6 **longevity**
(lŏn-jĕv′ĭ-tē)
-*noun*

- Volvos and Hondas are known for their **longevity**, often outlasting more expensive cars.
- The animal with the greatest **longevity** is the giant land tortoise, which can live several hundred years.

b *Longevity* means   a. form.   b. life span.   c. size.

7 magnitude
(măg′nĭ-tōōd′)
-*noun*

- Numbers in the billions and trillions are of too great a **magnitude** for most people to grasp.
- When the bank teller realized the **magnitude** of his error, he panicked at the thought of being held responsible for the loss of so large a sum of money.

_a_ *Magnitude* means   a. amount.   b. time.   c. length.

8 mundane
(mŭn-dān′)
-*adjective*

- Because Usha teaches belly dancing every day, it is simply one more **mundane** activity to her.
- The most **mundane** activities can turn into extraordinary events. For instance, I met my best friend while washing my clothes at the laundromat.

_c_ *Mundane* means   a. exciting.   b. painful.   c. commonplace.

9 obscure
(ŏb-skyōōr′)
-*adjective*

- The chemist didn't express his theory clearly, so it remained **obscure** to all but a few scientists.
- The police easily discovered who committed the murder, but even to the best psychiatrists, the killer's motives remained **obscure**.

_b_ *Obscure* means   a. unimportant.   b. unclear.   c. known.

10 render
(rĕn-dər′)
-*verb*

- Don't let the baby near your term paper with that crayon, or she will **render** it unreadable.
- Phyllis added so much red pepper to the chili that she **rendered** it too hot for anyone to eat.

_b_ *Render* means   a. to remember.   b. to make.   c. to wish.

Matching Words with Definitions

Following are definitions of the ten words. Clearly write or print each word next to its definition. The sentences above and on the previous page will help you decide on the meaning of each word.

1. _____*dispel*_____   To drive away as if by scattering; cause to vanish

2. _____*magnitude*_____   Size

3. _____*mundane*_____   Ordinary; everyday

4. _____*explicit*_____   Stated or shown clearly and exactly

5. _____*ambivalent*_____   Having conflicting feelings about someone or something

6. _____*render*_____   To cause (something) to become; make

7. _____*obscure*_____   Not easily understood; not clearly expressed

8. _____*aloof*_____   Cool and reserved; distant in personal relations

9. _____*augment*_____   To increase; make greater, as in strength or quantity

10. _____*longevity*_____   Length of life

CAUTION: Do not go any further until you are sure the above answers are correct. Then you can use the definitions to help you in the following practices. Your goal is eventually to know the words well enough so that you don't need to check the definitions at all.

➤ Sentence Check 1

Using the answer line provided, complete each item below with the correct word from the box. Use each word once.

a. **aloof**	b. **ambivalent**	c. **augment**	d. **dispel**	e. **explicit**
f. **longevity**	g. **magnitude**	h. **mundane**	i. **obscure**	j. **render**

_____ *mundane* _____ 1. The best writers can describe something ___ so that it doesn't seem ordinary at all.

_____ *augment* _____ 2. The architect decided to add another pillar to the building to ___ its support.

_____ *ambivalent* _____ 3. "Russell seems ___ toward me," Janice said, "as if he both likes and dislikes me."

_____ *longevity* _____ 4. Recent research suggests that our parents' ___ doesn't necessarily affect how long we will live.

_____ *aloof* _____ 5. When I'm frightened, I try to appear ___ because looking cool and distant helps me feel in control.

_____ *obscure* _____ 6. The essence of my science teacher's genius is that he is able to make complicated, ___ ideas clear to students.

_____ *render* _____ 7. "If you keep walking on the backs of your shoes like that, you will ___ them as flat as the floor," Annie's mother said.

_____ *dispel* _____ 8. If Claude proposes marriage to Jean, he will ___ any doubts she may still have as to whether or not he really loves her.

_____ *explicit* _____ 9. "I try to make my test questions as ___ as possible," said Mr. Baines, "so that my students will know exactly what answers I'm looking for."

_____ *magnitude* _____ 10. I began to realize the ___ of the insect population when I read that there are more kinds of insects living today than all other kinds of animals in the world.

NOTE: Now check your answers to these questions by turning to page 128. Going over the answers carefully will help you prepare for the next two practices, for which answers are not given.

➤ Sentence Check 2

Using the answer lines provided, complete each item below with **two** words from the box. Use each word once.

_____ *longevity* _____
_____ *explicit* _____ 1–2. When asked about his ___, ninety-year-old Mr. Greene gives an ___ recipe for a long life: eat well, exercise, and stay away from hospitals. "It's ironic°," he explains, "that I got the worst infection of my life at a hospital."

_____ *augment* _____
_____ *magnitude* _____ 3–4. Harried was able to ___ the family income by working overtime, but her problems with her husband and children increased in ___.

ambivalent
render

5–6. I'm ___ about playing with our rock band. The music is a source of elation° for me, but I'm afraid it will ___ me deaf one of these days.

aloof
dispel

7–8. Gail sometimes appears cold and conceited, but she is ___ only toward people she strongly dislikes. With all others, her usual genial° and modest manner soon ___s any impression that she is overly proud.

obscure
mundane

9–10. "Does the idea that we don't always see things as they really are seem ___ to you?" the teacher asked. "If so, it will become clearer if you relate it to the ___ experience of looking down a road. Doesn't it look narrower in the distance than it really is?"

➤ _Final Check:_ **My Sister's Date**

Here is a final opportunity for you to strengthen your knowledge of the ten words. First read the following selection carefully. Then fill in each blank with a word from the box at the top of the previous page. (Context clues will help you figure out which word goes in which blank.) Use each word once.

I watched as my older sister, Ruth, removed the last spiked curler from her hair. We gaped° at the result. She somehow had (1)_____ _render_ _____(e)d her hair limp as spaghetti. When Ruth started to cry, I tried to pacify° her with my usual gentleness: "Why are you such a crybaby about some stupid guy?"

The guy was Steven Meyer. He and Ruth were going to a high school dance. She'd had a crush on him for years, for reasons that were (2)_____ _obscure_ _____ to me. (I never had been able to discern° what she saw in him.)

When Ruth began to (3)_____ _augment_ _____ her makeup by applying some more powder, she gave a terrifying scream that probably reduced my (4)_____ _longevity_ _____ by at least a year. She informed me between sobs that a pimple had just appeared on her nose, making her "look like a vile° witch." I studied her face, expecting a pimple of truly amazing (5)_____ _magnitude_ _____. Instead, I spotted a tiny speck. I tried to (6)_____ _dispel_ _____ Ruth's worries: "So, it makes you look like a witch. Don't you want to look bewitching?" But she just began to cry again. I took this opportunity to go downstairs and wait for Steven Meyer.

He arrived a half hour before Ruth was ready. Observing him through my thick glasses, I tried to figure out exactly what Ruth saw in him. We talked until she appeared at the top of the stairs. Trying to look (7)_____ _aloof_ _____, she came down very slowly, wearing a cool, distant expression.

When Ruth returned home later that night, her comment about the evening was (8)_____ _explicit_ _____: "Totally rotten." She said that Steven, far from being extraordinary, had turned out to be "the most (9)_____ _mundane_ _____ sort of person in the world." It seemed Ruth had bypassed feeling (10)_____ _ambivalent_ _____ about Steven and gone straight from love to hate.

It's just as well, since I've been married to Steven for ten years now.

| _Scores_ | Sentence Check 2 _____% | Final Check _____% |

Enter your scores above and in the vocabulary performance chart on the inside back cover of the book.

UNIT FOUR: Review

The box at the right lists twenty-five words from Unit Four. Using the clues at the bottom of the page, fill in these words to complete the puzzle that follows.

Word box:

- aloof
- avid
- constrict
- cryptic
- depict
- dispel
- esteem
- fallible
- feasible
- feign
- furtive
- gape
- implicit
- ironic
- legacy
- mundane
- muted
- obscure
- pacify
- pragmatic
- pretentious
- punitive
- render
- saturate
- vile

ACROSS

1. Suggested but not directly expressed
5. Cool and reserved; distant in personal relations
8. Practical
9. Ordinary; everyday
11. To make smaller or narrower, as by squeezing or shrinking
12. Capable of making an error
15. Making a show of excellence or importance, especially when undeserved
19. To pretend; give a false show of
21. Opposite to what might be expected
22. Softened; toned down, made less intense
23. To drive away as if by scattering; cause to vanish
24. Offensive to the senses, feelings, or thoughts; disgusting

DOWN

2. Something handed down from people who have come before
3. Having a vague or hidden meaning; puzzling
4. To stare in wonder or amazement, often with one's mouth wide open
6. Possible; able to be done
7. To make calm or peaceful
10. Not easily understood; not clearly expressed
13. Enthusiastic and devoted
14. To represent in pictures or words; describe
15. Giving or involving punishment; punishing
16. High regard; respect; favorable opinion
17. To soak or fill as much as possible
18. Done or behaving so as not to be noticed; secret; sneaky
20. To cause (something) to become; make

UNIT FOUR: Test 1

PART A
Choose the word that best completes each item and write it in the space provided.

_____habitats_____ 1. Endangered species won't survive unless their ___ are preserved.

      a. inhibitions   b. habitats   c. precedents   d. esteems

_____explicit_____ 2. Peter hasn't been ___ about quitting his job, but he's hinted at it.

      a. explicit   b. transient   c. fallible   d. punitive

_____precedent_____ 3. I didn't let the kids stay up late last night because I didn't want to set a(n) ___ for future nights.

      a. longevity   b. habitat   c. inhibition   d. precedent

_____implicit_____ 4. When my brother complained of a shortage of cash, his ___ message was "Can you lend me some money?"

      a. punitive   b. vindictive   c. implicit   d. aloof

_____condoned_____ 5. Rosa has ___ her son's temper tantrums for so long that he thinks they're acceptable behavior.

      a. feigned   b. rendered   c. dwindled   d. condoned

_____esteem_____ 6. The poker gang laughed when Mom asked to join their game, but their ___ for her rose as she won the first four hands.

      a. esteem   b. longevity   c. legacy   d. magnitude

_____formulated_____ 7. While driving home three hours after her curfew, Lucille ___ an excuse she hoped her parents would believe.

      a. ruptured   b. gaped   c. formulated   d. saturated

_____exhaustive_____ 8. After a(n) ___ search during which I crawled around my entire apartment, my "missing" contact lens fell out of my eye.

      a. exhaustive   b. furtive   c. implicit   d. vindictive

_____ironic_____ 9. It's ___ that my rich uncle is so stingy and my parents, who aren't rich, are always lending money to family members.

      a. exhaustive   b. ironic   c. furtive   d. pragmatic

_____feigned_____ 10. Although he had heard about his grandmother's aches and pains a million times, Dennis ___ interest whenever she complained to him.

      a. dwindled   b. feigned   c. constricted   d. pacified

(Continues on next page)

<u>   *depicted*   </u>   11. In talking with the social worker, the abused child ___ a life of horror.

        a. depicted   b. rendered   c. mediated   d. saturated

<u>   *pretentious*   </u>   12. Dean is so ___ that he refers to his position of hamburger cook at a fast-food restaurant as "chef."

        a. feasible   b. transient   c. pretentious   d. muted

PART B

Write **C** if the italicized word is used **correctly**. Write **I** if the word is used **incorrectly**.

  I   13. *Saturate* the washcloth by wringing it out.

  C   14. Eating sticky dried fruits can be as *detrimental* to your teeth as eating candy.

  C   15. Female elephants join together to help each other *nurture* their young.

  I   16. In a surprisingly *punitive* mood, our boss let everyone off early last Friday.

  C   17. The suspect had such a *furtive* expression that he appeared to be hiding something.

  I   18. Mort's back talk *pacified* his father, who then denied him the use of the car for a month.

  C   19. After our truck ran over a sharp rock, a tire *ruptured*. Luckily, we had a spare in the trunk.

  I   20. My grandfather's *pathetic* gardening won him two first prizes in the state flower show.

  C   21. I have to ignore Jesse completely now to *dispel* any idea he may have that I'm romantically interested in him.

  I   22. In the package, pantyhose look so small that it's hard to believe they'll *constrict* enough to fit over a woman's legs and hips.

  C   23. The poem is *obscure* because it jumps from one complicated image to another.

  C   24. I don't consider cooking an entire meal a *mundane* task because I do it so rarely.

  I   25. When a friend broke her expensive china bowl, Harriet remained *genial*, yelling, "If I had known you were so clumsy, I would have used paper plates."

> ***Score***   (Number correct) _____ x 4 = _____ %

Enter your score above and in the vocabulary performance chart on the inside back cover of the book.

UNIT FOUR: Test 2

PART A

Complete each item with a word from the box. Use each word once.

a. aloof	b. ambivalent	c. contemplate	d. fallible
e. feasible	f. fiscal	g. inhibition	h. legacy
i. magnitude	j. muted	k. reconcile	l. render

muted   1. To make the bright green a more ___ shade, the painter added a few drops of black.

render   2. Cooking vegetables for too long ___s them less nutritious.

aloof   3. Inez may seem ___, but she's not cold once she gets to know you.

contemplate   4. Why ___ dropping out of school when you've got only two semesters to go?

ambivalent   5. Isabel has ___ feelings about her job. She loves the work but hates her boss.

magnitude   6. No one realized the ___ of Nora's depression until she tried to kill herself.

feasible   7. It isn't ___ to grow roses in our back yard. There's too much shade back there for roses.

legacy   8. My love of the outdoors is a(n) ___ from my grandfather, who often hiked in the mountains.

inhibition   9. At first, Tiffany was reluctant to sit in Santa Claus's lap, but she overcame her ___s when she saw that he was handing out candy canes.

fiscal   10. The company is in such bad ___ shape that over half the employees will soon be laid off.

reconcile   11. As the wedding drew near, Brenda had to ___ herself to the fact that her son would marry a woman she disliked.

fallible   12. To remind everyone that we're all ___, my boss keeps on his desk a giant eraser imprinted with the words "For Big Mistakes."

(Continues on next page)

PART B
Write **C** if the italicized word is used **correctly**. Write **I** if the word is used **incorrectly**.

_C_   13. Karen found the chicken salad *vile*. One small taste made her gag.

_I_   14. I asked Sal to *augment* the stereo because it was giving me a headache.

_C_   15. Some spiders have surprising *longevity,* living as long as twenty years.

_I_   16. The Changs' *transient* marriage has already lasted over fifty years.

_C_   17. When the *vindictive* tenant moved out, he broke all the windows in his apartment.

_I_   18. Being a *pragmatic* person, my brother values music and poetry more than practical things.

_C_   19. An *avid* reader, Judy spends much of her time enjoying newspapers, magazines and books.

_C_   20. My liking for my supervisor *dwindled* as his temper grew shorter and his list of "don'ts" grew longer.

_I_   21. Fascinated by the cartoon on TV, the little boy *gaped* at his mother as she left for work.

_C_   22. If a flamingo is *deficient* in a type of vitamin A, its feathers won't turn pink.

_I_   23. As Dad left for work, he called out his usual *cryptic* comment: "See you later."

_I_   24. Nate *mediated* a fight with his sister by calling her boyfriend "pickleface."

_C_   25. Music in a minor key often *evokes* sad feelings in the listener.

Score   (Number correct) _____ x 4 = _____ %

Enter your score above and in the vocabulary performance chart on the inside back cover of the book.

UNIT FOUR: Test 3

PART A: Synonyms
In the space provided, write the letter of the choice that is most nearly the **same** in meaning as the **boldfaced** word.

_c_ 1. **saturate** a) burst b) make c) soak d) scatter

_d_ 2. **gape** a) look for b) notice c) see d) stare

_b_ 3. **condone** a) forbid b) put up with c) encourage d) imitate

_c_ 4. **vindictive** a) practical b) complete c) vengeful d) surprising

_a_ 5. **contemplate** a) think about b) decide c) prefer d) wait

_d_ 6. **ambivalent** a) active b) sure c) not harmful d) having mixed feelings

_d_ 7. **esteem** a) curiosity b) disapproval c) acceptance d) respect

_c_ 8. **legacy** a) promise b) example c) inheritance d) increase

_a_ 9. **feign** a) pretend b) conceal c) develop d) oppose

_b_ 10. **habitat** a) hobby b) environment c) lifestyle d) diet

_c_ 11. **longevity** a) youth b) good health c) life span d) death

_d_ 12. **pacify** a) care for b) encourage c) admire d) calm down

_c_ 13. **formulate** a) recognize b) aim for c) develop d) promote

_c_ 14. **rupture** a) accept b) draw forth c) burst d) fill as much as possible

_a_ 15. **implicit** a) suggested b) in conflict c) devoted d) brief

_b_ 16. **precedent** a) effect b) earlier example c) goal d) main cause

_c_ 17. **dispel** a) recognize b) oppose c) drive away d) create

_b_ 18. **inhibition** a) something handed down b) holding back c) tone d) wish

_d_ 19. **magnitude** a) favorable opinion b) length of life c) location d) importance

_b_ 20. **render** a) scatter b) cause to become c) increase d) make narrower

_c_ 21. **fiscal** a) generous b) physical c) economic d) expensive

_b_ 22. **depict** a) select b) describe c) ignore d) expect

_a_ 23. **pretentious** a) acting important b) fictional c) practical d) well-off

_d_ 24. **evoke** a) increase b) make narrow c) reply d) bring forth

_c_ 25. **mundane** a) unlikely b) ridiculous c) commonplace d) harmful

(Continues on next page)

PART B: Antonyms

In the space provided, write the letter of the choice that is most nearly the **opposite** in meaning to the **boldfaced** word.

_b_ 26. **pragmatic**   a) mistaken   b) impractical   c) offensive   d) untalented

_a_ 27. **aloof**   a) friendly   b) mean   c) handsome   d) ambitious

_d_ 28. **constrict**   a) admire   b) build   c) accept   d) make wider

_a_ 29. **pathetic**   a) admirable   b) possible   c) broad   d) safe

_c_ 30. **avid**   a) quiet   b) rare   c) unenthusiastic   d) impractical

_b_ 31. **detrimental**   a) pleasant   b) helpful   c) respectful   d) clear

_a_ 32. **augment**   a) decrease   b) oppose   c) deny   d) avoid

_c_ 33. **furtive**   a) wise   b) successful   c) unhidden   d) impossible

_a_ 34. **muted**   a) brightened   b) corrected   c) forbidden   d) out in the open

_b_ 35. **deficient**   a) kind   b) having enough   c) useful   d) permanent

_d_ 36. **punitive**   a) in favor of   b) organized   c) straightforward   d) rewarding

_b_ 37. **transient**   a) frequent   b) permanent   c) rare   d) possible

_b_ 38. **dwindle**   a) replace   b) increase   c) reveal   d) improve

_d_ 39. **exhaustive**   a) poorly stated   b) boring   c) impractical   d) incomplete

_d_ 40. **reconcile**   a) contrast   b) accept   c) cause to vanish   d) decide to reject

_c_ 41. **nurture**   a) dislike   b) win   c) neglect   d) fail to notice

_a_ 42. **fallible**   a) perfect   b) beautiful   c) understandable   d) willing

_c_ 43. **explicit**   a) poorly supported   b) lengthy   c) vague   d) complicated

_b_ 44. **ironic**   a) strong   b) expected   c) true   d) covering few details

_d_ 45. **vile**   a) organized   b) permanent   c) large   d) pleasant

_b_ 46. **feasible**   a) manageable   b) impossible   c) surprising   d) delayed

_d_ 47. **cryptic**   a) suggested   b) everyday   c) kind   d) clear

_c_ 48. **genial**   a) not typical   b) impractical   c) unfriendly   d) foolish

_a_ 49. **mediate**   a) prevent agreement   b) recognize   c) forget   d) be active

_c_ 50. **obscure**   a) brief   b) disorganized   c) easily understood   d) correct

Score   (Number correct) _____ x 2 = _____%

Enter your score above and in the vocabulary performance chart on the inside back cover of the book.

UNIT FOUR: *Test 4*

PART A
Complete each sentence in a way that clearly shows you understand the meaning of the **boldfaced** word.
Take a minute to plan your answer before you write.

Example: To increase your **longevity**, _exercise frequently and avoid alcohol, tobacco, and high-fat foods_.

1. **Pragmatic** Ramona spends her money on such things as _____*(Answers will vary.)*_____

   _____.

2. One thing the nursery-school teacher did to **nurture** each child each day was _____

   _____.

3. The critic summed up how **pathetic** the actor's performance was with this comment: " _____

   _____."

4. The car accident **rendered** Philip _____

   _____.

5. The **magnitude** of Carol's musical talent became clear to us when _____

   _____.

6. A student **deficient** in study skills might _____

   _____.

7. We learned how **fallible** the house builder was when _____

   _____.

8. I have had to **reconcile** myself to the fact that _____

   _____.

9. When he wasn't invited to the wedding, the bride's **vindictive** cousin _____

   _____.

10. I'm such an **avid** fan of _____ that I'll _____

    _____.

(Continues on next page)

PART B

After each **boldfaced** word are a *synonym* (a word that means the same as the boldfaced word), an *antonym* (a word that means the opposite of the boldfaced word), and a word that is neither. On the first answer line, write the letter of the word that is the synonym. On the second answer line, write the letter of the word that is the antonym.

　　　　Example: _a_ _b_ **dwindle**　　a. lessen　　　b. increase　　　c. turn

_c_ _b_ 11–12. **aloof**　　　　a. angry　　　b. friendly　　　c. reserved

_a_ _c_ 13–14. **detrimental**　　a. harmful　　b. organized　　c. beneficial

_c_ _a_ 15–16. **punitive**　　　a. rewarding　b. requiring　　c. punishing

_a_ _b_ 17–18. **transient**　　　a. brief　　　b. permanent　　c. lively

_c_ _a_ 19–20. **explicit**　　　a. vague　　　b. loud　　　c. clear

PART C

Use five of the following ten words in sentences. Make it clear that you know the meaning of the word you use. Feel free to use the past tense or plural form of a word.

| a. **condone** | b. **contemplate** | c. **esteem** | d. **feign** | e. **furtive** |
| f. **gape** | g. **habitat** | h. **inhibition** | i. **pacify** | j. **vile** |

21. _____ *(Answers will vary.)* _____

_____

22. _____

_____

23. _____

_____

24. _____

_____

25. _____

_____

Score　(Number correct) _____ x 4 = _____%

Enter your score above and in the vocabulary performance chart on the inside back cover of the book.

A. Limited Answer Key

Important Note: Be sure to use this answer key as a learning tool only. You should not turn to this key until you have considered carefully the sentence in which a given word appears.

Used properly, the key will help you to learn words and to prepare for the activities and tests for which answers are not given. For ease of reference, the title of the "Final Check" passage in each chapter appears in parentheses.

Chapter 1 (Joseph Palmer)

Sentence Check 1

1. adamant
2. encounter
3. malign
4. amiable
5. amoral
6. epitome
7. absolve
8. antagonist
9. animosity
10. eccentric

Chapter 2 (A Cruel Sport)

Sentence Check 1

1. tangible
2. obsolete
3. acclaim
4. adjacent
5. escalate
6. engross
7. exploit
8. methodical
9. terminate
10. elicit

Chapter 3 (No Luck with Women)

Sentence Check 1

1. mercenary
2. allusion
3. altruistic
4. assail
5. euphemism
6. taint
7. appease
8. syndrome
9. arbitrary
10. banal

Chapter 4 (Accident and Recovery)

Sentence Check 1

1. calamity
2. ponder
3. flagrant
4. comprehensive
5. conventional
6. persevere
7. rehabilitate
8. turmoil
9. fluctuate
10. venture

Chapter 5 (Animal Senses)

Sentence Check 1

1. enhance
2. attest
3. dispatch
4. exemplify
5. enigma
6. nocturnal
7. discern
8. orient
9. mobile
10. attribute

Chapter 6 (Money Problems)

Sentence Check 1

1. predominant
2. concurrent
3. constitute
4. prerequisite
5. nominal
6. decipher
7. recession
8. default
9. confiscate
10. hypothetical

Chapter 7 (The New French Employee)

Sentence Check 1

1. suffice
2. sinister
3. vulnerable
4. intricate
5. implausible
6. sanctuary
7. incoherent
8. scrutiny
9. degenerate
10. intercede

Chapter 8 (A Cruel Teacher)

Sentence Check 1

1. immaculate
2. blight
3. gloat
4. blatant
5. contrive
6. garble
7. retaliate
8. gaunt
9. qualm
10. plagiarism

Chapter 9 (Learning to Study)

Sentence Check 1

1. Intermittent
2. devastate
3. incorporate
4. indispensable
5. incentive
6. rigor
7. squander
8. curtail
9. digress
10. succumb

Chapter 10 (The Mad Monk)

Sentence Check 1

1. intrinsic
2. alleviate
3. virile
4. cynic
5. infamous
6. covert
7. revulsion
8. speculate
9. benefactor
10. demise

Chapter 11 (Conflict Over Holidays)

Sentence Check 1

1. aspire
2. benevolent
3. diversion
4. mandatory
5. abstain
6. deficit
7. dissent
8. affiliate
9. agnostic
10. lucrative

Chapter 12 (Dr. Martin Luther King, Jr.)

Sentence Check 1

1. Conversely
2. extrovert
3. poignant
4. prevalent
5. contend
6. proponent
7. charisma
8. contemporary
9. traumatic
10. quest

Chapter 13 (Relating to Parents)

Sentence Check 1

1. prone
2. congenial
3. flippant
4. prompt
5. rapport
6. impasse
7. relentless
8. perception
9. reprisal
10. rationale

Chapter 14 (The Nightmare of Gym)

Sentence Check 1

1. detract
2. ominous
3. averse
4. elation
5. nullified
6. endow
7. expulsion
8. disdain
9. divulge
10. mortified

Chapter 15 (A Model Teacher)

Sentence Check 1

1. waive
2. commemorate
3. deplete
4. transcend
5. complacent
6. niche
7. menial
8. diligent
9. consensus
10. empathy

Chapter 16 (Shoplifter)

Sentence Check 1

1. gape
2. contemplate
3. precedent
4. feasible
5. condone
6. fiscal
7. furtive
8. pathetic
9. feign
10. punitive

Chapter 17 (A Nutty Newspaper Office)

Sentence Check 1

1. deficient
2. rupture
3. ironic
4. detrimental
5. inhibition
6. depict
7. vindictive
8. cryptic
9. saturate
10. implicit

Chapter 18 (Roughing It)

Sentence Check 1

1. vile
2. genial
3. reconcile
4. constrict
5. formulate
6. exhaustive
7. Pretentious
8. habitat
9. pragmatic
10. fallible

Chapter 19 (Getting Scared)

Sentence Check 1

1. pacify
2. evoke
3. dwindle
4. muted
5. nurture
6. transient
7. esteem
8. avid
9. legacy
10. mediate

Chapter 20 (My Sister's Date)

Sentence Check 1

1. mundane
2. augment
3. ambivalent
4. longevity
5. aloof
6. obscure
7. render
8. dispel
9. explicit
10. magnitude

B. Dictionary Use

It isn't always possible to figure out the meaning of a word from its context, and that's where a dictionary comes in. Following is some basic information to help you use a dictionary.

HOW TO FIND A WORD

A dictionary contains so many words that it can take a while to find the one you're looking for. But if you know how to use guide words, you can find a word rather quickly. *Guide words* are the two words at the top of each dictionary page. The first guide word tells what the first word is on the page. The second guide word tells what the last word is on that page. The other words on a page fall alphabetically between the two guide words. So when you look up a word, find the two guide words that alphabetically surround the word you're looking for.

• Which of the following pair of guide words would be on a page with the word *skirmish*?

(**skimp** / **skyscraper**)   **skyward** / **slave**   **sixty** / **skimming**

The answer to this question and the questions that follow are given on the next page.

HOW TO USE A DICTIONARY LISTING

A dictionary listing includes many pieces of information. For example, here is a typical listing. Note that it includes much more than just a definition.

> **driz•zle** (drĭz′əl), *v.*, **-zled, -zling,** *n. — v.* To rain gently and steadily in fine drops. — *n.* A very light rain. —**driz′zly,** *adj.*

Key parts of a dictionary entry are listed and explained below.

Syllables. Dots separate dictionary entry words into syllables. Note that *drizzle* has one dot, which breaks the word into two syllables.

• To practice seeing the syllable breakdown in a dictionary entry, write the number of syllables in each word below.

gla•mour __2__   **mic•ro•wave** __3__   **in•de•scrib•a•ble** __5__

Pronunciation guide. The information within parentheses after the entry word shows how to pronounce the entry word. This pronunciation guide includes two types of symbols: pronunciation symbols and accent marks.

Pronunciation symbols represent the consonant and vowel sounds in a word. The consonant sounds are probably very familiar to you, but you may find it helpful to review some of the sounds of the vowels—*a, e, i, o,* and *u.* Every dictionary has a key explaining the sounds of its pronunciation symbols, including the long and short sounds of vowels.

Long vowels have the sound of their own names. For example, the *a* in *pay* and the *o* in *no* both have long vowel sounds. Long vowel sounds are shown by a straight line above the vowel.

In many dictionaries, the *short vowels* are shown by a curved line above the vowel. Thus the *i* in the first syllable of *drizzle* is a short *i*. The pronunciation chart on the inside front cover of this book indicates that the short *i* has the sound of *i* in *sit*. It also indicates that the short *a* has the sound of *a* in *hat*, that the short *e* has the sound of *e* in *ten*, and so on.

• Which of the words below have a short vowel sound? Which has a long vowel sound?

drug __short__   **night** __long__   **sand** __short__

Another pronunciation symbol is the *schwa* (ə), which looks like an upside-down *e*. It stands for certain rapidly spoken, unaccented vowel sounds, such as the *a* in *above,* the *e* in *item,* the *i* in *easily,* the *o* in *gallop,* and the *u* in *circus.* More generally, it has an "uh" sound, like the "uh" a speaker makes when hesitating. Here are three words that include the schwa sound:

in•fant (ĭn′fənt)   **bum•ble** (bŭm′bəl)   **de•liv•er** (dĭ-lĭv′ər)

• Which syllable in *drizzle* contains the schwa sound, the first or the second? _____*second*_____

Accent marks are small black marks that tell you which syllable to emphasize, or stress, as you say a word. An accent mark follows *driz* in the pronunciation guide for *drizzle,* which tells you to stress the first syllable of *drizzle.* Syllables with no accent mark are not stressed. Some syllables are in between, and they are marked with a lighter accent mark.

• Which syllable has the stronger accent in *sentimental*? _____*third*_____

sen•ti•men•tal (sĕn′tə-mĕn′tl)

Parts of speech. After the pronunciation key and before each set of definitions, the entry word's parts of speech are given. The parts of speech are abbreviated as follows:

noun—*n.*   pronoun—*pron.*   adjective—*adj.*   adverb—*adv.*   verb—*v.*

• The listing for *drizzle* shows that it can be two parts of speech. Write them below:

_____*noun*_____   _____*verb*_____

Definitions. Words often have more than one meaning. When they do, each meaning is usually numbered in the dictionary. You can tell which definition of a word fits a given sentence by the meaning of the sentence. For example, the word *charge* has several definitions, including these two: **1.** To ask as a price. **2.** To accuse or blame.

• Show with a check which definition (1 or 2) applies in each sentence below:

The store charged me less for the blouse because it was missing a button.   1 _✓_   2 ___

My neighbor has been charged with shoplifting.   1 ___   2 _✓_

Other information. After the definitions in a listing in a hardbound dictionary, you may get information about the *origin* of a word. Such information about origins, also known as *etymology,* is usually given in brackets. And you may sometimes be given one or more synonyms or antonyms for the entry word. *Synonyms* are words that are similar in meaning to the entry word; *antonyms* are words that are opposite in meaning.

WHICH DICTIONARIES TO OWN

You will find it useful to own two recent dictionaries: a small paperback dictionary to carry to class and a hardbound dictionary, which contains more information than a small paperback version. Among the good dictionaries strongly recommended are both the paperback and the hardcover editions of the following:

The American Heritage Dictionary
The Random House College Dictionary
Webster's New World Dictionary

ANSWERS TO THE DICTIONARY QUESTIONS
Guide words: *skimp/skyscraper*
Number of syllables: 2, 3, 5
Vowels: *drug, sand* (short); *night* (long)
Schwa: second syllable of *drizzle*

Accent: stronger accent on third syllable *(men)*
Parts of speech: noun and verb
Definitions: 1; 2

C. Word List

absolve, 8
abstain, 68
acclaim, 12
adamant, 8
adjacent, 12
affiliate, 68
agnostic, 68
alleviate, 54
allusion, 16
aloof, 114
altruistic, 16
ambivalent, 114
amiable, 8
amoral, 8
animosity, 8
antagonist, 8
appease, 16
arbitrary, 16
aspire, 68
assail, 16
attest, 24
attribute, 24
augment, 114
averse, 80
avid, 110
banal, 16
benefactor, 54
benevolent, 68
blatant, 46
blight, 46
calamity, 20
charisma, 72
commemorate, 84
complacent, 84
comprehensive, 20
concurrent, 38
condone, 98
confiscate, 38
congenial, 76
consensus, 84

constitute, 38
constrict, 106
contemplate, 98
contemporary, 72
contend, 72
contrive, 46
conventional, 20
conversely, 72
covert, 54
cryptic, 102
curtail, 50
cynic, 54
decipher, 38
default, 38
deficient, 102
deficit, 68
degenerate, 42
demise, 54
depict, 102
deplete, 84
detract, 80
detrimental, 102
devastate, 50
digress, 50
diligent, 84
discern, 24
disdain, 80
dispatch, 24
dispel, 114
dissent, 68
diversion, 68
divulge, 80
dwindle, 110
eccentric, 8
elation, 80
elicit, 12
empathy, 84
encounter, 8
endow, 80
engross, 12

enhance, 24
enigma, 24
epitome, 8
escalate, 12
cstccm, 110
euphemism, 16
evoke, 110
exemplify, 24
exhaustive, 106
explicit, 114
exploit, 12
expulsion, 80
extrovert, 72
fallible, 106
feasible, 98
feign, 98
fiscal, 98
flagrant, 20
flippant, 76
fluctuate, 20
formulate, 106
furtive, 98
gape, 98
garble, 46
gaunt, 46
genial, 106
gloat, 46
habitat, 106
hypothetical, 38
immaculate, 46
impasse, 76
implausible, 42
implicit, 102
incentive, 50
incoherent, 42
incorporate, 50
indispensable, 50
infamous, 54
inhibition, 102
intercede, 42

Notes

Notes